_1995_

Americans of Italian Heritage

Margherita Marchione

University Press of America, Inc.
Lanham • New York • London

Copyright © 1995 by
Margherita Marchione
University Press of America,® Inc.
4720 Boston Way
Lanham, Maryland 20706

3 Henrietta Street
London, WC2E 8LU England

Library of Congress Cataloging-in-Publication Data

Marchione, Margherita.
Americans of Italian heritage / Margherita Marchione.
p.   cm.
Includes index.
1. Italian Americans--Biography.   I. Title.
E184.I8M278   1995
920'.009251--dc20   94-41101 CIP

ISBN 0-8191-9825-0 (cloth: alk paper)
ISBN 0-8191-9826-9 (pbk: alk paper)

⊖™The paper used in this publication meets the minimum
requirements of American National Standard for Information
Sciences—Permanence of Paper for Printed Library Materials,
ANSI Z39.48–1984

This book is lovingly dedicated to

Eileen and N. Larry Paragano

CONTENTS

INTRODUCTION

This volume memorializes the accomplishments of key figures among the Italian-Americans of the twentieth century. They are the descendants of Italian immigrants and, through their achievements, bear witness to the sacrifice and valor of their forefathers.

The men and women featured are different from one another in personality and profession. They are contemporary people, highly energetic and intensely involved in achieving their goals and making a contribution to the

American dream. They have the capacity to inspire others by their dedication, and strive to help build and shape our nation.

Italian-American history did not begin with the great immigrations of the nineteenth and twentieth centuries. It began with the discovery of the new world half a millennium ago, when Christopher Columbus forged a path that millions of Italian immigrants have since followed. Because of their courage, we are able today to reaffirm the principles for which the Constitution stands and to pay tribute to the documents that guarantee our rights and freedoms.

Italian influence pervaded all facets of life in the American colonies and manifested itself in the arts, the social refinements, and cultural pursuits, as well as in the realm of philosophical and political ideas.

Undoubtedly, the United States has been enriched by the heritage of this ethnic group that, through its explorers and immigrants, brought with them the literature of Dante Alighieri, the art of Michelangelo Buonarotti, and the music of Antonio Vivaldi and Giuseppe Verdi.

Early on, Italians ventured into the unknown areas and expanded geographical knowledge. In the seventeenth century Italian explorers, in the service of Spain, England, Portugal and France, devoted their lives and fortunes to the creation of America. Venetian glassmakers settled in Jamestown, Virginia, and farmers from Piemonte settled in the Delaware. Others migrated to Savannah, Georgia, for the production of silk.

Like Columbus, all were courageous; all had dreams to fulfill. In the eighteenth century another dreamer, Philip

Mazzei, arrived in Virginia on his chartered ship, The "Triumph." Little did he dream, however, that he would be the founder of "The Constitutional Society of 1784," and the first Italian to arrange commercial relations beyond the Atlantic. His writings give us an eyewitness account of the three great national upheavals of the late eighteenth century —the American and the French revolutions, and the events which led to the second partition of Poland. Mazzei's message exemplifies the spirit of sacrifice, the courage, and the hope of our forefathers.

Italian-American organizations have been active in changing and enhancing the image of Italians in America. Among the more prominent organizations are UNICO National and the National Italian American Foundation.

In 1922, UNICO National was started in Connecticut. It is patterned after service clubs similar to Lions and Kiwanis, but different in that it is composed of American citizens of Italian origin. Based on the principle of "Service Above Self," it is an organization that develops friendship and leadership.

In 1975, in anticipation of the Bicentennial Celebrations, the National Italian American Foundation was established in Washington, D.C. It fulfilled the dream of millions of Italian-Americans throughout the United States. It not only represented their hopes and aspirations but also recognized their achievements.

Dedicated to preserving the Italian heritage and its values by integrating them into the mainstream of American life, the NIAF has become a national catalyst for the work and achievements of social, fraternal and service organizations on the local level.

This book is a record of people who possess considerable interest in their particular fields. It documents their remarkable contribution to society and their devotion to Italian heritage and culture that provides inspiration to succeeding generations. They are recipients of the Lifetime Achievement Awards presented by the NIAF. The list also includes two outstanding Italians—Sophia Loren and Gian Carlo Menotti—whose association with and activities in the United States of America have been exceptional.

All the profiles honor individuals of national and international reputation and celebrity. Their stories portray the spirit and commitment of people who make history and serve humanity. Their careers reflect the entire spectrum of American society and culture.

When President George Bush issued a proclamation designating the month of October as "Italian-American Heritage and Culture Month," he spoke of the extraordinary contributions Italian-Americans have made to our life as a Nation: "Whether defending freedom on the front lines of battle or participating in the daily workings of our democracy, Italian-Americans have clearly demonstrated their love of freedom and self-government and their profound respect for the rights and dignity of every individual. Their patriotism—coupled with their deep faith and devotion to family life—has truly strengthened the fabric of our society."

In his first Columbus Day Proclamation, President Bill Clinton recognized the courage and vision of the discoverer of America. As President, he called upon the people of the United States to observe the day with appropriate ceremonies and activities. "Americans of international descent, along with Native Americans," he added, "have contributed mightily to molding the framework of our great land, united by our allegiance to the principles of equality, democracy, and freedom."

Italian-Americans take justifiable pride in the men and women who dedicated their lives to the pursuit of their dreams. Future generations will reflect on the accomplishments of the many individuals who were recognized by the National Italian American Foundation for their achievements. Posterity will celebrate their unique talents, capture their spirit, and emulate their commitment to society.

Margherita Marchione
Villa Walsh
Morristown, NJ 07960-4928

Danny Louis Aiello, Jr.

Danny Aiello, the actor with an incredibly unorthodox past, spent his early childhood in New York City until the family moved to the relatively countrified atmosphere of Boston Road in the Bronx. His mother, Frances Pietrocova from Naples, Italy, had married Daniel Aiello when she was fifteen.

Danny and his six siblings were raised almost singlehandedly by their mother. From his childhood, he worked an endless series of jobs including selling newspapers and shining shoes at Grand Central Station. As a teenager, he served a three-year stint in the Army, where he was stationed in Germany. Returning to the United States, he married Sandy Cohen, "the most beautiful girl in the Bronx." He became so caught up in a decidedly working-class existence that being an actor was far from his mind.

When he was laid off from his position as the President of the Greyhound Bus Union, Aiello landed a job as a bouncer at New York's Comedy Club, "The Improvisation," and began to fill-in as an emcee. Though he had never seen a play, he reasoned that acting would be an interesting career.

A lifelong resident of New York, Danny Aiello began acting in his mid-'30s and set the tone for his career by immediately earning a Theater World Award for his debut in *Lamppost Reunion*. With absolutely no formal training, his award-winning debut performance led to a number of prominent theater credits including *Knockout,* Woody Allen's *The Floating Light Bulb,* and *The House of Blue Leaves.*

With a reputation for no-holds-barred stage and screen performances which are brimming with honest emotion, Aiello's portrayal of Cher's jilted fiance in *Moonstruck* endeared him to film audiences. As Sal in controversial director Spike Lee's *Do The Right Thing,* Aiello received unanimous acclaim including Academy Award and Golden Globe nominations for Best Supporting Actor. He was also named Best Supporting Actor by the Los Angeles, Boston and Chicago Film Critics Associations.

Aiello received an Obie Award for his starring role in *Gemini*—a role he later recreated on Broadway. He also received a Fabergé Award and two Jefferson nominations for *That Championship Season.* Additionally, he won unanimous critical acclaim and a LADCC Best Actor Award for his "on-the-edge" portrayal of Phil in the L.A. debut of *Hurlyburly.*

After making his motion-picture debut in *Bang The Drum Slowly,* Aiello continued to distinguish himself in such feature films as *Hide in Plain Sight, Once Upon A Time in America* and *The Purple Rose of Cairo,* among others. On television, he received an Emmy Award for Best Actor for his work in the M.O.W. *A Family of Strangers.*

A respected actor whose services are in constant demand, Aiello was acclaimed for Buena Vista's *The Cemetery Club.* He stars as Ben Katz, a Pittsburgh widower who meets three widows (Ellen Burstyn, Olympia Dukakis and Diane Ladd) at a cemetery where they are each visiting their spouses' graves. The role offers Aiello the opportunity not only to play a romantic lead, but also to show off his dancing abilities.

Aiello was seen in Columbia Pictures' *The Pickle,* directed by Paul Mazursky and scheduled for release. He stars as a Jewish American filmmaker who struggles for his art, only to find success when he is forced to make a commercial film in order to survive. In addition, Aiello appears in *Mistress,* with Robert DeNiro.

The actor was also seen in Propaganda Films' *Ruby,* starring as Lee Harvey Oswald's murderer, Jack Ruby. *Ruby* is a probing inquiry into the world of organized crime and the destruction of a man whose actions catapult him from obscurity to international notoriety.

Aiello starred in Twentieth Century Fox's *29th Street,* portraying an exasperated father unable to believe the luck of his youngest offspring. He received raves from the critics for this performance, as well as for his portrayal of family patriarch Joe Bella in *Once Around,* with Richard Dreyfuss and Holly Hunter.

Commenting on Aiello's inauspicious beginning but almost meteoric rise, fellow-actor Elliot Kouver remarked: "At first I felt sorry for him. Then a year after he became an actor, I spotted his name on a Broadway marquee ... above the title!"

At a black-tie dinner in his honor, Danny Aiello recalled how his devoted mother supported her family and publicly thanked her, as well as his loving wife, Sandy, for providing "the wind beneath my wings." His mother's faith in him and his wife's love and support helped ignite the raw talent that has been refined and tempered with the years. His acting technique has developed with instinct, inspiration and hard work. Critics have praised his characterizations for being authoritative, gripping, and immensely disciplined. Woody Allen recognized his consummate artistry when he called him "simply a natural."

Aiello rejected several lucrative offers for television series and syndicated miniseries in favor of screen and stage roles because, in his own words, "I want to continue to do important work in features—make each role I take count. You just can't do that on television no matter how good the initial intention."

In short, Aiello wants to leave his personal stamp in the mind of his viewers and to be remembered by them for his sensitivity and compassion and, hopefully, "to be loved by the greatest number of people it is humanly possible to be loved by."

Certainly, he has felt and been inspired by the warmth of fans, colleagues and critics alike. He must have been warmed by a great measure of collective love in 1989, particularly, when he not only was honored by the National Italian American Foundation with its Lifetime Achievement Award, but also chosen to be the Grand Marshal of the Columbus Day Parade in his beloved New York City.

Though his work tends to take him away from home for extended periods of time, Danny Aiello remains firmly rooted in New York and to his wife Sandy and their four children, Rick, Danny III, Jaime and Stacey.

References: *Current Biography,* H.W. Wilson & Co., June 1992.
New York Times Magazine, January 2, 1990.
People Magazine, February 18, 1990.

Alan Alda

Alan Alda, the internationally acclaimed actor-writer-director of stage, screen and television, may well owe his versatility to his eclectic background: Italian on his father's side and Irish on his mother's. His father, Robert Alda, was himself a distinguished actor and his mother was Joan Browne.

Growing up in New York City and in constant contact with his paternal grandparents (D'Abruzzo), he easily and happily assimilated their culture, their dreams, their philosophy, and tempered them with his own. Although never directly a butt of ethnic discrimination during his high-school years, he did become acutely aware of its prevalence when Joe, his best schoolfriend, told him of his many unfortunate brushes with it. He concluded that such bigots just had to be ignorant and were not worth worrying about. But still, the Alda of today remarks, "I never forgot the quiet, pained look in Joe's eyes when he told me."

A few years later, Alda had ample opportunity to learn more about his Italian heritage when, as a junior at Fordham University, he studied in Europe. Part of that year was spent performing on the stage in Rome and television in Amsterdam with his father. After graduation from Fordham (1956), he acted at the Cleveland Playhouse on a Ford Foundation Grant and then returned to New York where he appeared on Broadway, off-Broadway, as well as on television. Most beneficial to his career at that point was the improvisational training he received with "Second City" in New York and "Compass" at Hyannisport. This initiation into political and social satire led to his regular appearance on T.V.'s highly successful "That Was the Week That Was."

Alan Alda's major breakthrough to the Broadway stage came with his starring role in *The Owl and the Pussycat*. After that, he appeared in *Purlie Victorious*, in *Fair Game for Lovers*—for which he received a Theater World Award—and *The Apple Tree,* which earned him a Tony nomination.

Alda is recognized also for numerous memorable performances in such films as *Gone Are the Days* (1963), *Paper Lion* (1968), *Jenny* (1970) and later, *California Suite* (1978), *Same Time Next Year* (1978) and the award-winning *Crimes and Misdemeanors* (1989). He wrote and acted in *The Seduction of Joe Tynan* (1979); wrote, directed and acted in *The Four Seasons* (1981), *Sweet Liberty* (1986), *A New Life* (1987), and *Betsy's Wedding* (1990).

But it was television that gave this multi-faceted artist the greatest scope for his creative talents. Thus, in *M*A*S*H,* he not only starred as the unforgettable Dr. Benjamin Franklin "Hawkeye" Pierce, but he also wrote and directed many of the episodes. For television, too, he directed, staged and appeared in *6 Rms Riv Vu* (1974) which co-starred Carol Burnett, and in the Marlo Thomas Television Specials *Free To Be Me...You and Me* (1974). A year later he created, wrote, and co-produced the television series *We'll Get By,* and with Martin Bregman co-produced *The Four Seasons,* a T.V. series based on the hit film in which he had previously co-starred. Alda mentions that he was inspired to write on that theme by Vivaldi's haunting "Four Seasons" composition.

Incredibly Alan Alda still finds the time and energy to participate actively in causes and organizations he believes in. He campaigned ardently and extensively for ten years for the passage of the Equal Rights Amendment. In 1976, President Gerald Ford acknowledged his commitment by appointing him to the National Commission for the Observance of International Women's Year.

Alda is a Trustee of the Museum of Broadcasting and also of the Rockefeller Foundation. His achievements have been acknowledged with multiple awards from the prestigious Directors' Guild of America, the Writers' Guild of America, and the Screen Actors' Guild.

Winning awards, however, is not confined to the man of the Alda household. He is extremely proud of his wife, Arlene Weiss Alda, a professional photographer who has won many awards for her work, which has appeared in numerous magazines, including *Life, Vogue, People, U S,* and *Ms.;* she has also written six books which have been very well received. Each of these two creative people is obviously proud and supportive of the other and devoted to their three daughters—Eve, Elizabeth and Beatrice.

Alda's deep respect and love for his family was touchingly expressed in his talk during the National Italian American Foundation Awards Dinner when he accepted its Life Achievement Award. He spoke nostalgically of his close-knit family, of Sunday gatherings of the clan at his grandparents' house in Queens, and of his abiding pride in Italian culture and Italian achievements in the arts, the sciences, explorations and the like.

His pride does not end there, he emphasized; it isn't all based on glorious achievements and geniuses. For him, there is something more. "I have a simple, very personal sense of being Italian," he explained; "it's the love of life, the love of eating, of laughing, the love of love itself. I have seen in Italy a sense of dignity, a sense of humor, and a sense of physical grace and comic expressiveness all rolled into one character trait that is irresistible...an utterly accepting love of improvisation that welcomes each new day. ... Every problem is an opportunity for human contact, for play. And if not for play, then at least for unbridled emotion. I love life so, therefore, I love being Italian."

References: Ephraim Katz, *The Film Encyclopedia*, Putnam Publishing Co., 1982.
Who's Who in Entertainment, 1989.

Joseph Antonini

Sometimes referred to as the Lee Iacocca of retailing, Joseph Antonini has been chairman and CEO of Kmart corporation since 1987. He has chosen to be a hands-on, highly visible and committed supervisor and director. His achievements are all the more impressive since, in the course of his service, Kmart has become the second largest retailer in the United States.

This is no surprise to those who watched Antonini grow up in Morgantown, West Virginia, where he was born on July 13, 1941. Even as a youngster, he earned a reputation for doing difficult things with energy, style and against seeming odds. For example, being relatively short did not prevent him from becoming the star guard on the Morgantown High School basketball team.

Later, while matriculating at the University of West Virginia, he formed a rock-and-roll group, the Bonnevilles, to help pay for his tuition. When he could not afford the sound equipment to compete with what the other groups used, Antonini devised a different ploy to attract the crowds: he carefully studied the charts and selected the songs that were high on the lists and were bringing in the most money.

In 1964, Antonini was taken on by S.S. Kresge (now Kmart), as a management trainee at Troy, Michigan. Since then he has worked his way up steadily through more than a dozen positions and promotions in the corporation before reaching his present station. By the late 1960s, Kmart was dazzling its investors and the buying public with stores that featured discount prices and spacious layouts—both innovative features for those days.

Some twenty years later, by which time Antonini had become chief operating officer and, subsequently, chief executive officer, he and the senior managers turned their attention to other operational areas and diverted cash flow by buying such disparate enterprises as Waldenbooks (now the nation's largest bookstore chain), PayLess Drug stores, the Builders Square home-repair chain and the Pace Membership Warehouse Clubs. All have proven to be excellent investments but Pace is expected to realize the most spectacular growth of all. Keeping in step with innovations overseas, Kmart, in partnership with Bruno's, the Alabama food retailer, opened an American counterpart of the "Hyper-marché"—its American Fare; it combines a supermarket's food and a discount store's clothing and houseware merchandise.

Yet expansion and diversity have not been Antonini's only concerns, especially since he became President of Kmart in 1987. He has been taking great pains to purge Kmart of its "polyester palace" image, by adding more expensive merchandise to low-priced lines and recruiting a bevy of celebrities to hawk certain merchandise. Thus Mario Andretti endorses Kmart's automotive products. Martha Stewart, the up-scale caterer, plugs products for the kitchen, bedroom or bath.

The most successful of such marketing coups so far has involved Jaclyn Smith, an "Angel" of T.V. fame. The moderately priced line of women's clothing she touts has obviously responded to a crying need of Kmart's women customers: they want something a little classier than polyester and they are willing to pay for it. As the Mustang revitalized Ford many years ago, Jaclyn Smith's line of clothing has worked comparable wonders for Kmart. It helped turn the $6 billion apparel division into Kmart's fastest-growing business and move it closer to Antonini's goal—to entrench it as a leader, not merely a follower or copier, in retail female apparel.

Not content to rest on his laurels, Antonini turned his efforts to implementing a $2.5 billion effort to modernize all 2200 of the stores and make them more cost-efficient by introducing such improvements as wider aisles, better lighting, clearer signs and improved inventory control. To remain competitive, Kmart must not only improve its technology and renovate existing stores, but also add new ones in spite of the current economic doldrums. It also proposes to add more name-brand merchandise and reduce the prices, thus realizing a considerable increase in revenue.

Antonini's contribution to Kmart's projected expansion and up-scaling are not all made at his desk or at meetings: he does considerable legwork and first-hand study and observation, as well. He averages eight to ten visits to Kmart stores a week, for off-the-cuff talks with employees and clientele, to assess the climate, the trends, the needs of the moment and of the particular marketing situation.

Frequently, he stops in at some competitors' stores. This keeps him informed about just which merchandise people are favoring or refusing, which articles might be introduced to advantage and which would make the most money into the bargain.

The information and ideas derived from such visits are translated into products, presentations and procedures as

soon as feasible. Thus, for example, are the recently introduced petite-size line for women, the expanded inven-
tory in cosmetics, jewelry and children's clothing and the
significant price reduction on thousands of Kmart's more
popular items. As he breezes through the various stores,
he also takes scrupulous note of whether the merchandise
is displayed to advantage, or if the stockroom is overly
supplied for true effectiveness.

Antonini has also bowed to the inevitable—the TV
commercial; in genial chitchats with customers and personnel he has familiarized the buying public with the various facets of the Kmart enterprise. However, Antonini is
acutely aware that, although a commercial may lead the
consumer to the sales counter, he might not ultimately
purchase the product in question if the sales person doesn't
do his part of the work efficiently. Accordingly, Kmart
has developed a comprehensive training program for all
its associates. It is called Path to Excellence and it deline-
ates and stresses the benefits of outstanding customer service and customer-oriented job skills. Several of these
new programs are credited not only with honing skills but
also with reducing staff turnover considerably.

Antonini proudly explains that Kmart personnel are
recruited without discrimination and from non-traditional
sources, including people with disabilities and seniors. "We
provide inner-city youth with job-training, career counsel-
ing and a position in a local store. Our future strength lies
in our associates."

Today, with the competition increasing in numbers and aggressiveness and the national economy so unpredictable, Antonini's work impinges more than ever on his personal life. Since he is generally in his office at 6:00 a.m. during the work week, the time he can spend at home with his wife, Kathleen, and their children, John and Kara, is curtailed. Yet, given his professional expertise in time-and-quality efficiency, the choice times he and his family spend together are undoubtedly satisfying and rewarding.

In 1989, Antonini received the NIAF Business Community Award and, in 1992, the President of the Republic of Italy conferred on him the prestigious *Commendatore* Award of the Italian order of Knighthood.

References: *Businesss Week,* October 21, 1988 and October 7, 1991.
Fortune Magazine, April 15, 1988 and January 2, 1989.
Harvard Business Review, November-December 1991.
Hoover's Handbook of American Business, 1992.
Marketing, April 1991.
The Wall Street Journal, January 22, 1992.

Brian Boitano

Brian Boitano, the 1988 champion figure-skater who won the first gold medal in that competition for the United States, could well be a role model for young Americans willing and prepared to work relentlessly in their specialties, even at the cost of great personal sacrifices.

Born in Mountain View, California (October 22, 1963), Brian was the youngest of the four children of Donna and Lew Boitano. Although it is a closely knit family to this day, it wasn't until the Olympics in Calgary, in February 1988, that they were all able to attend any of his performances together. That is one of the necessary sacrifices of an internationally active career. His father is his financial adviser and his mother handles most of his mail; they are an integral part of what they call "Team Boitano."

Brian's ice-skating career began at eight years old, after he was inspired by a performance by the Ice Follies. Initially, he began taking group lessons with Linda Leaver as the instructor. She soon realized his potential and became his coach, then his personal manager. At fourteen, while still in high school, he became the U.S. Junior Men's Champion.

At nineteen, Brian gained world recognition, as the first skater to complete all six different triple jumps in a World Championship. In the 1984 Olympic Winter Games in Sarajevo, he placed fifth; subsequently, he won the first of four consecutive U.S. Men's titles in 1985.

Just one year before his triumph at the Winter Olympics in Calgary, Canada, he improvised a unique jump, the Tano Triple, never completed by any other skater. Just one month after the Olympics, he defended and won the World Figure-Skating Title in Budapest, Hungary, with an unprecedented seven perfect marks: it was the first time a skater had been judged to have perfectly executed the most difficult elements possible under the rules.

Boitano turned professional in 1988, and remains the undefeated world professional champion, having placed first and scored perfect tens in all nine of the professional championships he has entered. Singlehandedly, he has changed the face of professional figure-skating, raising its standard beyond any already established level in the history of that sport. Many writers consider him superior to any other figure-skater of the past or present. He does not sacrifice his expression of feeling and emotion during the most difficult routines. He explains: "Ice is to me what a canvas is to a painter. My life has been about creating on ice."

As a professional, Brian became the first American male athlete to have his own network television special, "Brian Boitano: Canvas of Ice," which was shown on ABC in December 1988. This critically acclaimed special won awards in the International Film and Television Festival of New York and the Chicago International Film Festival.

Then Boitano turned to a medium he had not yet explored—films. He teamed up with the German skater, Katarina Witt, to star in a full-length feature film titled *Carmen on Ice* (HBO). Filmed in Seville and Berlin and enhanced and accompanied by the music of the Vienna Symphony Orchestra, it was enthusiastically received by public and critics alike. In fact, both stars won an Emmy for the "Outstanding Individual Performance in the Performing Arts." In particular, the critics commended Boitano for flawlessly executing the most difficult moves while at

the same time communicating his feelings. Unquestion-
ably, he had brought new dimensions to his skating-danc-
ing and acting.

In the winter of 1990, Boitano and Witt organized
their own tour with an international cast of twelve world-
class skaters. *Skating,* as it was billed, toured successfully
twenty-eight cities in North America. *Skating II,* its all-
new sequel, was equally well received in its performances
in Portland, Baltimore, and some thirty other cities, always with a minimum of props and a maximum of athletic and dancing artistry.

Boitano's performances in these and previous ventures,
as an amateur and as a professional, inspired the *San
Francisco Chronicle* (December 29, 1990) to proclaim
him the Michael Jordan of ice-skating and to recognize in
him "a spirited sense of play, a delight that never seems
exhibitionistic or vain. He rises above the technique, labor, and danger of his sport without seeming smug or
arrogant about it. You can't take your eyes off Brian
because you can't wait to see what inspiration will seize
him next."

Although he is at his peak, Boitano is aware of the
inexorable wages of time and is beginning to contemplate
a non-skating future: "When I get to be forty years old and
can't do a triple axel any more, I don't want to go on the
ice." He hopes to open a restaurant in San Francisco, his
hometown; he dreams of performing in musical comedy
on Broadway. He has kept a journal since 1980 and has
an autobiography in mind.

of some peripheral hard-won distinctions as well: he was the first foreign-born Mayor of Cleveland, Ohio, and the first non-native to be appointed to the U.S. Cabinet, and as a judge to the U.S. Court of Appeals.

Anthony was born, September 4, 1910, to Rocco and Dorothy Marcogiuseppe Celebrezze in Anzi, a village in Potenza, Italy. The ninth of thirteen children, he was but two years of age when the family migrated to this country.

His father, Rocco Celebrezze, worked for the railroad as a track walker, and found it difficult to provide for his sizable family. Young Anthony at six was selling newspapers along with his brothers at a downtown stand in Cleveland which became known as "Celebrezze Corner." He continued pulling his share throughout his elementary school years, and most of high school. During his senior year at Central High he played halfback and also increased the family's income by boxing on local sports programs.

After graduation he studied at John Carroll University in Cleveland for a year and then transferred to Ohio Northern University in Ada. To support himself he loaded freight and labored on section gangs for the New York Central Railroad.

He received a LL.B. degree in 1936 and was admitted to the Ohio Bar. After three years on the legal staff of the Ohio Bureau of Unemployment Compensation, he entered general practice, opening his own law office where he worked for the next 13 years, except for a stint in the Navy during World War II.

His political career was launched in 1950, when he was elected to the Ohio Senate in the Democratic Party, and re-elected in 1952. He distinguished himself by his exemplary service on such crucial committees as the Judiciary, Taxation, Veteran's Affairs, and Civil Defense. He was twice voted one of the top Senators during his terms of office. Celebrezze's political career gained even greater momentum when in 1953, as an independent Democrat, he ran for the office of Mayor of Cleveland. He was re-elected to that office four times, and in 1961, when he ran for the fifth time, he received an unprecedented 73.8% of the total vote and carried every one of Cleveland's thirty-three wards. His main objectives during those five terms were to achieve mutual understanding and co-operation among the communities, to clear the slums, develop the Erieview Project, and make Cleveland a world port with the development of the St. Lawrence Seaway.

His distinction as the only mayor in the history of Cleveland to be elected to five consecutive terms can be ascribed to his earnestness and energy in working closely with people, as well as with complex administrative problems. Mayor Celebrezze was demonstrably concerned for the welfare of the physically handicapped, for refugees, and for those facing forcible relocation. His competence as mayor was acknowledged not only by his constituents and his associates, but also by the American Municipal Association when it elected him as President in 1958, and by the U.S. Conference of Mayors when it, too, elected him President in 1962.

The vast variety and scope of Judge Celebrezze's activities include the Salvation Army Centennial Citation; Eleanor Roosevelt Humanities Award; United Negro College Fund Award for leadership on behalf of Greater Education Opportunity for American Youth; Award of Merit, National Council of Senior Citizens; Expression of Deep Appreciation, from United Negro College Fund; B'nai Brith Award for Promoting Harmony and Brotherhood; Central High School Restoration Committee's Prestigious Alumnus Award, in local, state and national government, and in honor of character, leadership, and wisdom (March 10, 1991).

In addition to the innumerable other awards, honorary college degrees and testimonials to his admirable achievements, Judge Celebrezze has been honored in a spectacular way by the Jewish National Fund of Cleveland; in his honor they have planted a grove of one thousand trees in the American Bicentennial National Park in the State of Israel, in recognition of his outstanding public service as a statesman and jurist.

In like recognition and appreciation, the United States Congress, by an act passed July 20, 1974, ruled the new Federal building in Cleveland be known as the Anthony J. Celebrezze Federal Building.

In private life, Anthony J. Celebrezze has been married since May 7, 1938, to his high-school sweetheart, Anne Marco, a graduate of Western Reserve University, and former teacher in the Cleveland public-school system. They have three children—Anthony Jr., Attorney-at-Law and former Attorney General, State of Ohio; Jeanne Anne Porto of Washington, D.C., and Susan Maria Sullivan, a librarian in the School of Law of Boston College.

References: *Current Biography,* H.W. Wilson & Co., 1963.
The New Columbia Encyclopedia, Columbia University Press, 1975.
Who's Who in the Midwest, 1960.

joined the Marriott Corporation. He steadily climbed the corporate ladder through hard work, professional vision and enterprise. He is credited with contributing to a twenty-fold increase in Marriott's business, which had become the #1 hotel for customer preference.

Despite his achievements, in time Checchi determined that being the CEO of a large corporation was not what he really wanted. He was primarily interested in something more entrepreneurial. In 1982, he teamed up with Bass Brothers of Fort Worth, Texas, as a financial strategist. He soon figured in lucrative deals Bass made with Texaco, Inc., with Arvida Corp., and with Walt Disney Co., where he served as an adviser to the Disney chairman on financial restructuring, real estate development and strategic planning. "Focusing only on making money can make one miss what business should be all about. It is about building things," he remarked. He credits Walt Disney and Marriott with this awareness. Accordingly, in 1986, he launched out on his own and later started the Alfred Checchi Association, Inc., of which he is still president. This Los Angeles consulting firm oversees investment portfolios and acquisition programs.

Within three years of initiating his own company, Checchi realized that the greatest public service he could perform was being an accomplished and people-oriented executive, motivating large numbers of associates and employees, creating, negotiating and implementing suitable strategies for the benefit of all. But he realized that he would need "partners"—a track team. He carefully and gradually gathered together the "friends" with whom he chose to work in this new enterprise. This concept has undoubtedly contributed to the smooth relationship within the ranks of the vast organization—Northwest Airlines, based in St. Paul, Minnesota. In 1989, Checchi and Gary L. Wilson, another former Marriott Corporation executive, led a group of investors in a four-billion-dollar-plus leveraged buy-out of Northwest Airlines—the fourth largest in the United States.

Alfred Checchi proudly claims that his organization has never lost sight of its four defined objectives: To be the best place to work; to be the best provider of services for customers; to be the best managed; and, finally, to measure up as a great corporate citizen. This involves honoring its responsibilities not only to customers, but to employees, communities, the aviation industry as a whole, and to the country as well. Illustrating just one of these objectives, Checchi has pointed out that during the Gulf War, when all the airlines felt the pinch and some responded by laying off personnel, Northwest absorbed the losses and kept all its people working.

Unlike many of its competitors, Northwest has weathered the economic crisis and still has enough financing options to keep flying. However, Checchi sees only one viable strategy for Northwest in these difficult times: "To broaden its reach through alliances with foreign airlines, to assure long-term success and to expand, or be an also-ran." Considering past performances and achievements,

Perry Como

Perry Como, the Italian-American crooner with the deceptively relaxed manner, who wound up being "King of the Jukes" and a star of radio and television, was born in Canonsburg, Pennsylvania, May 18, 1912. His parents, Pietro and Lucia Como, had both emigrated from Italy in the early 1900's. His father was a mill hand for Standard Tin Plate Corporation.

Perry, who was baptized Pierino, was one of thirteen children. To help ease his parents' financial burden, he began working after school in a barber shop at age eleven. Within a few years he was paying installments on his own shop, but his father compelled him to finish school first. At twenty-one, he owned his shop. He ran his business for six years, also becoming adept at barbershop singing. Encouraged by friends, he went to Cleveland to audition for Freddy Carlone's orchestra and was hired as a singer. He and his bride, the former Roselle Belline, toured with the band through the Midwest for three years.

In 1937, the popular orchestra leader, Ted Weems, signed him on. Six years later, when Weems joined the Army, the orchestra dispersed and Como returned to Canonsburg, fully intending to reopen his barber shop and enjoy his family, which now included a son, Ronald. However, before he had time to resume his business, he was offered the opportunity to appear on a CBS radio program. Ever the family man, Como accepted only after being assured that he would be permitted to live in New York for the duration of the program.

Shortly after, he was signed for a trial of two weeks at the highly popular Copacabana, the New York City nightclub. Although he faced the daunting competition of Frank Sinatra, Como measured up very well in the eyes of public and critics alike who saw in him a promising new star.

million and multi-million-selling records: a novelty song, "Papa Loves Mambo," a ballad, "Wanted." "Hot Diggity" and "Delaware," two novelty winners, and "More," still another ballad, were gold disc winners. "It's Impossible" in 1971, and "And I Love You So" in 1973, were also multi-million-selling albums. He continued to record, occasionally doing specials, guest spots or commercials on television; he remained consistently on the pop-music charts through 1973.

A highlight of his later career was his Grammy award for the Best Vocal Performance in his rendering of "Catch a Falling Star." After that were sporadic appearances, notably in the television presentation, "Cole Porter in Paris," and each time he broke attendance records and was enthusiastically received by fans and critics alike. Although he was in his late '60s when he began making world tours in the '80s, they were still being sold out in advance.

Perry Como has been one of the most commercially successful of all pop recording artists and vocalists. He has also found time to play a vital role in many ethnic and charitable events and to be one of the founders of the Hospitalized Veterans' National Radio Foundation. His favorite leisure activity? He has been known to say that he would rather play golf than sing.

Perhaps the most remarkable and least heralded achievement of this talented Italian-American singer is not merely his rise from rags to riches, his transition from small-town barber to universal superstar, but rather his obvious commitment to the ideals of family, home, integrity and privacy. Unlike many others in his fast-tracked profession, his way of life and his extra-professional activities and lifestyle have made poor grist for the scandalmongers' mill. As a result, both during his very active years and his present semi-retirement, he has succeeded in enjoying his family, his privacy and his chosen way of life.

References: *Baker's Biographical Dictionary of Musicians,* 7th ed., Nicholas Slonimsky, Macmillan, 1971.
Current Biography, H.W. Wilson, 1947.
Roger Kinkle, *The Complete Encyclopedia of Popular Music and Jazz, 1900-1950,* Arlington House Publishers, Westport, CT., 1974.
Hitchcock and Sadie, *The New Grove Dictionary of American Music,* Macmillan, London, 1989.
Norton-Grove, *Concise Encyclopedia of Music,* W.W. Norton & Co., 1988.
Arnold Shaw, *Dictionary of American Pop/Rock,* Schirmer Books, 1982.

In 1976, at the end of his ninth term in Congress, Dominick Daniels chose to return to Jersey City and re-enter private practice. He died eleven years later on July 17, 1987.

References: *Daily Record,* Northwest, NJ, July 22, 1987.
Who's Who in American Government, 1987.

Arthur J. Decio

Arthur J. Decio, currently Chairman of the Board and Chief Executive Officer of the Skyline Corporation of Elkhart, Indiana, was born in that city, October 19, 1930. His parents were Julius A. and Lena Alesia Decio. Young Arthur attended and was graduated from local schools

Joe Di Maggio

Joseph Paul Di Maggio—the greatest representative of Italian descent in the most popular American game, baseball—was born in Martinez, California, November 25, 1914. His parents, Paolo and Rosalia Di Maggio had emigrated from Isola delle Femmine, a small island off the coast of Palermo, Sicily. Paolo preceded his wife to the United States, working until he had accumulated enough money to send for her and their infant daughter, Nellie. Descended from generations of hard-working Sicilian fishermen, he worked at the same trade in his new country, as his family expanded to four girls and five boys. Two of the boys followed family tradition and became crab fishermen in the North Beach section of San Francisco; the other three, including next-to-the-youngest Joe, would become Major League baseball players.

After his freshman year in Galileo High School and his initiation into the school baseball team, even without the validation of an unaffordable uniform, Joe proved to himself that baseball was the answer for him. When his brother Vince was hired to play for the San Francisco Seals, Joe avidly followed the games through a knothole in the fence surrounding the field.

During the 1932 season, he was allowed to practice with them occasionally and replaced a retiring shortstop for the three remaining games. His first real break came when his brother Vince injured himself and Joe was chosen to replace him. From the very first day, as the story goes, "he covered the outfield like a tent." In the space of just one year, the 20-year-old rookie was acknowledged as the greatest player the Coast League had ever produced.

The Yankees signed him up in 1935, but accidents and injuries would bedevil him during his whole career. He

had to earn every penny we paid him," commented Del Webb, co-owner of the Yankees at the time.

Di Maggio again made the headlines on January 14, 1954, when he married Marilyn Monroe. The marriage ended in divorce within the year, but his love for her continued and after her death he was more reclusive than ever. He became vice-president of the Oakland A's and, in 1969, Joe Di Maggio was presented with the award for the Greatest Living Player. Although anything after that just had to be an anticlimax, he continued his work with the Oakland A's, finding profound satisfaction with "the kids", including Sal Bando, Rick Monday and Reggie Jackson who, as Di Maggio says, "couldn't catch a fly ball. Look at him now. He's about the best there is."

In 1984, he moved to South Florida, hoping that the climate would be easier on his arthritis. Initially, of course, his activities there centered on baseball, but he became more and more interested in golf, and has even participated in some tournaments with well-known golfers. Referring to this interest, he is quick to explain, "This is fun, but baseball was my life." He proved his credibility and persuasiveness before the T.V. cameras in his commercials for Mr. Coffee and the Bowery Savings Bank. He still strikes an impressive figure. Tall, lean and handsome with thick wavy white hair, there is a new softness to his expression now. He is ever impeccably groomed, polite, and with unstudied dignity. Yet the legendary *Joltin' Joe*, the *Yankee Clipper*, the *Big Guy* (as his teammates called him), is indelibly enshrined in memory and proudly evoked not only by baseball buffs, but also by his contemporaries who can readily recall the exciting headlines he made during those 13 glorious pennant years for the Yankees, as a superb hitter, base-runner and thrower.

Joe Di Maggio has been more formally honored along the years by countless organizations and societies, not only for his memorable statistics, but also for his humanity, his dignity, his modesty, and his well-proven sense of responsibility to family, to the young, to his country, and to his heritage.

In 1989, the NIAF presented him with its Lifetime Achievement Award. This was an impressive acknowledgment of both his extraordinary achievements and his Italian heritage, which contributed to his success with its commitment to hard work, persistence, and seemingly unattainable dreams.

References: Maury Allen, *Where Have You Gone, Joe Di Maggio?*
          E.P. Dutton & Co., 1975.
          Current Biography, 1941.
          Di Maggio, J., *Lucky to Be a Yankee,* 1946.
          Roger Kahn, *Joe and Marilyn,* William Morrow &
          Co., 1986.
          John Thorn-Peter Palmer, ed., *Total Baseball,*
          Warner Books, 1980.

Henry Fonda

Director Joshua Logan saw actor Henry Fonda as "a kind of synthesis of all the heroes of Mark Twain, Bret Harte, James Fenimore Cooper, Hawthorne, Poe and Irving." Fonda's fame derives from his performances in more than eighty motion-pictures, several spectacular stage roles and even in television serials and specials.

Henry Jaynes Fonda was born in Grand Island, Ne-
braska, the oldest of three children and the only son of
Wiliam Brace and Herberta (Jaynes) Fonda. His father
traced his ancestry to a titled Genoese family who settled
in the Netherlands around 1400. Two centuries later, the
descendants established the town of Fonda, in upper New
York State, which is still flourishing today.

When Henry was six months old, the Fondas moved
to Omaha, where he and his sisters grew up and where
their father owned and operated a printing company. After graduating from Omaha Central High School in 1923,
he enrolled at the University of Minnesota as a journalism
major. He had to work his way through school, however,
and after a stint as a trouble-shooter for the Northwestern
Bell Telephone Company, he took on a job directing sports
at a settlement house. This entailed coaching all the sports,
as well as playing on the basketball team; before long, he
was physically drained and unable to keep up his studies.
Inevitably, he had to drop out of college at the end of his
second year.

He returned to Omaha where he first became attracted
to the theater, thanks to the encouragement and guidance
of Dorothy Brando, a friend of the Fonda family and mother
of Marlon Brando. Henry auditioned for and won the
juvenile lead in Philip Barry's *You and I* at the Omaha
Community Playhouse, where he stayed for three seasons.
Between theatrical appearances, he worked intermittently
as a window dresser, garage mechanic, iceman and office
boy.

After a vaudeville tour in which he helped write dialogue for George Billings, the Lincoln impersonator, Fonda returned to the Omaha Community Playhouse as assistant director, set designer and finally as actor in Eugene O'Neill's *Beyond the Horizon*. In 1928, he joined the newly formed University Players Guild in Falmouth, Massachusetts, and was given a role in *The Jest*. Margaret Sullavan was usually Fonda's leading lady and, during the group's 1931 winter season in Baltimore, they were married on Christmas Day.

Meanwhile Fonda was given his first Broadway role in the Theater Guild production of Romain Rolland's *The Game of Love and Death*. This led to other walk-on parts until he landed a role in Leonard Sillman's *New Faces* revues at New York's Fulton Theater. Fonda's performance piqued the interest of motion-picture agent Leland Hayward, who invited him to Hollywood for a meeting with Walter Wanger, the movie producer. Because the film world did not interest him at all, he flippantly asked for a salary of $1000 a week, confident that this would squash the deal. To his astonishment, he was immediately given a contract for two pictures a year.

He made his motion-picture debut with Janet Gaynor in the film version of *The Farmer Takes a Wife*, which he had played to critical acclaim on Broadway. His rise in films was meteoric and within two years Fonda was an established Hollywood star. By the end of the decade, he was famous and sought after internationally. His basic

grass-root genuineness, his appealing vulnerability and con-
vincing fearlessness and integrity made him the ideal
"American" personality in the eyes of movie fans. Over
the next three years, Fonda made eight more films: the
most memorable, perhaps, was *You Only Live Once,* with
Sylvia Sidney, which one reviewer wrote was "acted with
terrifying honesty." Despite his overwhelming success in
Hollywood, Fonda returned to the stage periodically. When
he was reasonably assured of a future in Hollywood, Fonda
hastened back to Mount Kisco, New York, to rejoin the
Westchester Players in *The Virginian.*

After his return to Hollywood, Fonda made ten pictures in two years, among them the well-remembered
Jezebel and *Mad Miss Manton.* During this phase of his
career Fonda began his association with the director, John
Ford, who persuaded him to play the part of the *Young Mr.
Lincoln.* With his imposing height, long legs, honest looks,
sunken eyes, artificial wart, frock coat and stovepipe hat,
Fonda became the best embodiment of Lincoln. Critics
pronounced it his best characterization. Fonda had reached
the peak of his early Hollywood career.

In the screen version of John Steinbeck's novel, *The
Grapes of Wrath,* Fonda brilliantly epitomized the suffer-
ings and the indignities of the poor in the United States.
His superb characterization won him an Academy Award
nomination and many job offers. He came to regret the
seven-year contract he ultimately accepted with Twentieth
Century Fox; however, he was permitted to make a film

"on loan" to Paramount—*The Lady Eve*—and later released for *The Ox-Bow Incident,* which critics hailed as a
landmark in movie history.

Fonda enlisted as an apprentice seaman in the United
States Navy. He saw active duty in the Pacific as a quar-
termaster, third class, aboard a destroyer, and served as an
assistant operations and air-combat intelligence officer. He
earned a Bronze Star and a Presidential citation and, in
October 1945, was discharged as a lieutenant, senior grade.

Despite his success in *My Darling Clementine,* Fonda
felt the familiar tug of the New York stage and played the
title role in *Mister Roberts* for three years. The screen
version followed in 1955. He played the role 1700 times
and never tired of it. The comedy-drama must have been
close to his heart because of his own recent experiences in
the Pacific and the sensitive, frustrated young lieutenant
he portrayed was all the more engaging and credible.
Fonda won a Tony for it as Best Actor of the Season.

Fonda's interpretation of the ambitious young bank executive in *Point of No Return,* also pleased the critics and
Wolcott Gibbs of *The New Yorker* called it a "singularly
relaxed, touching and humorous performance." Fonda
continued the variegated pattern of his career for the next
20 years: stage appearances, road tours, screen roles and
even T.V. films and adventure series. To name a few: *War
and Peace, The Wrong Man,* and *Twelve Angry Men.* For
the latter, he won a Golden Bear Award at the International Film Festival in Berlin in 1957.

A few highlights of Fonda's prolific career during the last 30 years of his life are: his portrayal of Secretary of State Robert Leffingwell in Otto Preminger's version of the Allen Drury novel, *Advise and Consent;* his characterization of an American statesman in the movie version of Gore Vidal's play, *The Best Man;* his performance in *The Red Pony,* based on John Steinbeck's novella.

Fonda's tour de force as the famous liberal lawyer, Clarence Darrow, was a huge box-office success. The theater was always packed. However, a few nights before the slated closing, Fonda collapsed in his dressing room.

He underwent surgery for the implantation of a pacemaker and, within a few months, there was another sequence of screen, stage and television appearances. His final role was his ultimate achievement—an Academy Award in 1982, just before his death—as Norman Thayer, the feisty octogenarian in *On Golden Pond,* opposite the legendary Katharine Hepburn and his own daughter, Jane. The emotional chasm separating father and daughter in the film and his preoccupation with death became all the more gripping and moving in view of their off-screen lives. His widow, Shirlee Adams, enriched the last 17 years of his life when he turned to painting, sculpturing and photography, thus adding the final dimensions to the composite image of the tall, lanky figure whose implicit strength and contained dignity and reticence epitomized the American ideal.

References: *Current Biography,* H.W. Wilson, Co., 1992.
Jane Fonda, *T.V. Guide,* "Remembering Dad," January 11, 1992.
Ephraim Katz, *The Film Encyclopedia,* Putnam Publishing Group, 1982.
Who's Who in the Theater, 1972.

Robert Charles Gallo

Research scientist and virologist, Dr. Robert Gallo is known for having discovered and isolated the virus that is linked to leukemia, after many others had failed. He is also a co-discoverer, with Frenchman Dr. Luc Montagnier, of the AIDS virus.

There was little indication in his early years in Waterbury, Connecticut, where he was born March 23, 1937, that medicine and medical research were to become his all-absorbing professions. Nor did his parents, Francis Anton and Louise Mary Cianciulli from northern Italy, initially nurture such dreams for their only son. His father, a self-made metallurgist, owned his own welding company and avidly read technical journals to expand his knowledge and widen his technical horizons to the benefit of his business enterprise. His efforts were well rewarded and he and his wife were able to provide not only love, but comfort and security to Robert and his younger sister, Judith, for those important formative years.

Tragedy struck unexpectedly when Robert was thirteen years old; his sister contracted leukemia. She was treated by an early method of chemotherapy which brought about only a temporary remission. The family was devastated and demoralized by her death. Robert immersed himself in sports and broke his back playing basketball during his senior year at high school.

The family friend and pathologist, Dr. Marcus Cox, who had diagnosed his sister's ailment, took Robert under his wing during his long convalescence, deftly neutralizing the boy's acquired negativism toward medicine and science.

Indeed, as soon as he was able, young Robert began spending his Saturdays following Dr. Cox on his rounds at St. Mary's Hospital. As his admiration for the doctor grew, Robert lost his reservations about medicine, came to appreciate and become excited by its challenges and resolved to become a researcher and a doctor.

Gallo graduated from Providence College in Rhode Island in 1959, and entered Thomas Jefferson Medical College in Philadelphia.

After a trying stint on a pediatric leukemia ward, he abandoned the idea of clinical medicine forever. From that moment on, as he admitted in an interview *(U.S. News and World Report,* June 3, 1991), he made the laboratory his haven from "the dying and the dead."

While still a student, Gallo conducted experiments involving the growth of red-blood cells. Officials at the National Cancer Institute in Bethesda, Maryland, were impressed by his published account of that research and hired him in 1965 as a clinical associate.

In three short years he advanced to the post of senior investigator in the laboratory of human tumor-cell biology. Inevitably his research focused on studying leukocytes, not only because it was an exciting new field, but also because, as he readily admits, "Deep in the back of my cortex, was the memory of my sister's leukemia."

In 1978, the research pursued by Gallo and his staff bore fruit. One of the variants of his HTL (Human T-cell Leukemia) virus was identified as a cause of leukemia. This marked the first time that a cancer-causing virus had been found in humans. For that achievement, Gallo was honored with the Albert Lasker Award and a proliferation of invitations to lecture from the most prestigious organizations.

His next monumental research culminated in May of 1984 when Gallo and his team identified the Human T-cell Leukemia virus (HTLV-III B) as responsible for AIDS; they had also developed a blood test to screen for the disease. His celebrity skyrocketed even beyond scientific circles, and he was frequently dubbed "the father of human retro-virology," and credited with proving that a virus strain could cause deadly diseases in human beings.

However, controversy soon vitiated the great satisfaction they initially enjoyed. For a team of scientists at the Pasteur Institute in Paris, led by Professor Luc Montagnier, claimed prior discovery of the AIDS virus. Their virus, LAV, indeed, was proven virtually identical with Gallo's HTLV-III. They also asked for a patent on the blood test they claimed they had developed for AIDS and filed with the United States Patent Office seven months before Gallo had filed for one. The scientific dispute—one of the most vituperative in decades—abates periodically and then resurfaces and fuels again. Various individuals and organizations have tried to effect a compromise or, at the very least, a truce.

In 1986, Gallo and Montagnier and their respective teams were the co-recipients of the Albert and Mary Lasker Foundation Award that honored "their unique contributions to the understanding of AIDS."

The controversy seemed to have been finally resolved in 1987 when President Reagan and President Mitterand

of France helped orchestrate an agreement which desig-
nated both scientists as co-discoverers of the AIDS virus.
In addition, the United States and France agreed to split
the royalties on the AIDS test. They agreed that credit for
the discovery should be shared and that 80% of the royalties from the sale of AIDS antibody kits should go to a
new French and American AIDS Foundation dedicated to
research.

But the peace was short-lived and claims and counter-
claims, accusations and denials periodically flare up. In
the Fall of 1990, the National Institute for Health cleared
Gallo of taking away anything from the French. However, the investigation continued, although both the American team and the French did acknowledge each other's
crucial contributions and conclude that there was no serious doubt that both III B and LAV cause AIDS.

Research continues unabated. The ultimate goals are
still envisioned: a vaccine to prevent AIDS and halt its
transmission, and a successful treatment for what has been
called the "20th century's darkest epidemic."

Gallo and his team of thirty-odd researchers zealously
continue their work at the National Cancer Institute. Despite the tremendous nervous and physical energy expended
in his work, his presence belies the tensions. In his mid-
'50s, he is still slim and tall and looks more like a CEO
than a prototypical scientist.

He cannot spend as much time as he would like with
his wife, Mary Jane Hayes, and their children—Robert,
Charles and Marcus—but his home is his haven, his insu-

lation from frustrations, his place to unwind and to plan and write.

Gallo's latest book, *Virus Hunting,* was published in 1991; his next one undoubtedly is an embryo. Yet no matter how many discoveries, honors and accolades accrue to his credit, he is still driven to do more.

"The day I stop solving problems in science," Gallo told reporter Shannon Brownlee *(U.S. News and World Report,* June 3, 1991), "I can conclude that I have died. The more I do, the further I am away from death."

References: *Current Biography,* H.W. Wilson Co., 1986.
Newsweek, March 18, 1991; June 10, 1991.
Science, June 21, 1991; November 15, 1991;
February 21, 1992; April 3, 1992.
The New York Times, February 16, 1990;
October 6, 1990; March 2, 1992.

Robert A. Georgine

When Robert A. Georgine was elected chairman and CEO of the ULLICO Family of Companies on December 5, 1990, it was the culmination of almost thirty years of experience in the labor movement as well as a recognition of his extensive involvement with the employee benefits industry, with government, and with public interest organizations. Since 1974, he had also been serving as President of the Building and Construction Trades Department (AFL-CIO).

Born in Chicago, July 18, 1932, to Silvio and Rose Menzana Georgine, he studied at the University of Illinois and DePaul University. Subsequently he was apprenticed with Local #74 of the Wood, Wire and Metal Lathers' International Union (1953) but left to serve in the U.S. Army from 1955-57. Only five years after his military discharge, he began his climb to union executive in Chicago, where he was appointed Assistant Business Manager for the Lathing Foundation. Among the most significant positions he has held since then, besides his presidency, are: Chairman and CEO Union Labor Life Insurance Co. (1990-present); Secretary-Treasurer, Building and Construction Trades Department, AFL-CIO (1971); President, Wood, Wire and Metal Lathers' International Union (1970); International Representative, Wood, Wire and Metal Lathers' International Union (1964).

Robert Georgine has accumulated an impressive record by serving on labor committees: Vice President and Member of Executive Council, AFL-CIO (1985-present); AFL-CIO Standing Committee on Political Education, Legislation, Housing, International Affairs Subcommittee on Perestroika; as well as AFL-CIO Housing Investment Trust; Economic Policy Special Subcommittee on Trade, Standing Committee on Safety and Occupational Health, and the Joint Administrative Committee of the Plan for the

Settlement of Jurisdictional Disputes in the Construction Industry.

From 1976 to 1990, Georgine served on the Board of Directors or on the Executive Committee of a wide range of industry groups including Alliance to Save Energy, American Nuclear Energy Council, American Productivity and Quality Center, Atomic Industrial Forum, Conservation Foundation (formerly Resolve Center for Environmental Conflict Resolution), Federal Reserve Bank of Richmond, Gas Research Institute, Mutual Life Insurance Company of Washington, D.C., National Coordinating Committee for Multiemployer Plans, National Corporation for Housing Partnerships, National Housing Conference National Planning Association (Long Range Land Use Planning Committee, Union Labor Life Insurance Company).

Georgine's diversified activities and functions have entailed membership in, or service for, numerous and varied government and public interest organizations. Specifically, he was Director, Executive Committee member or Member of these organizations: Advisory Board on the Built Environment of the National Academy of Sciences, Advisory Committee to Harvard-MIT Joint Committee for Urban Studies, Center for National Policy, Citizens for Tax Justice, Coalition for Employment through Exports, Columbia University/McGraw Hill Lecture Program on Business and Society.

In addition, he served on the Committee for National Health Insurance, Committee for Peace and Security in the Gulf, Congress of U.S. Joint Economic Committee (Infrastructure), Electric Power Research Institute Advisory Council, Farmworkers' Justice Fund, Federal National Mortgage Association Advisory Committee, Gas Research Institute Advisory Council, Gas Research Institute Member-At-Large of the Board of Directors, Institute of Collective Bargaining and Group Relations, Inc., Jamestown Foundation, Labor Advisory Committee for Trade Negotiation and Trade Policy, National Building Museum, National Center for Productivity and Quality of Working Life, National Citizens Coalition for the Windfall Profits Tax, Co-Chairman, National Committee for Full Employment, National Environmental Development Association, National Institute of Building Sciences, National Italian American Foundation, National Labor Advisory Council for the March of Dimes, National Low Income Housing Coalition, National Resource Center for Consumers of Legal Services, National Trust for Historic Preservation, National Women's Political Caucus, The President's Committee on Employment of People with Disabilities, Seabee Memorial Scholarship Association Board of Directors, Socially Responsible Investments Fund, SRI Fund, U.S. Department of Labor ERISA Advisory Council, White House Conference on Handicapped Individuals.

Because of the scope and the quality of his service, Georgine has been honored with the following awards: Membership on the Presidential Commission on Efficiency and Cost of Government, in recognition of his long-standing interest in productivity and work place efficiency; Citation for service with distinction to the construction industry on four separate occasions by *Engineering News-Record;* Commendation by the U.S. Department of labor for his contribution to the nation's safety and health programs; The Brotherhood Award of the National Conference of Christians and Jews which was conferred on him twice by the Washington, D.C., chapter of the National Conferences of Christians and Jews; The National Labor-Management Achievement Award for the Citizen's Asthma Research Institute Hospital (1979); Man-of-the-Year Award of the International Guiding Eyes, Inc. (1979); Man-of-the-Year Award of the Joint Civic Committee of Italian-Americans in Chicago (1977); Four Freedoms Award of the Italian-American Labor Council (1983); Committee for Concerned Italian-Americans (1984); Distinguished Achievement Award of the National Italian American Foundation (1980); Member of the U.S. Delegation to the Inauguration of Pope John Paul I.

Author of numerous articles and reports on economic issues, Georgine is frequently called upon to speak at both industry-related and academic gatherings. His almost 30 years of experience in the labor movement, coupled with his extensive involvement with the employee-benefits industry and with government and public-interest organizations, give substance and authenticity to whatever he speaks or writes about related subjects and issues.

In private life, this super-achiever and eclectic orga-
nizer and union executive is the husband of the former
Mary Rita Greener and father of their four
children—Robert, Georgine, Rosemarie and Mary Beth.

In a Labor Day address at Washington, D.C.'s Sacred
Heart Cathedral (September 7, 1992), Georgine spoke about
Labor's service to the community at large. He maintains
that labor unions have directly benefited the community as
a whole through their charitable contributions, volunteer
activities and their fund-raising efforts to combat deadly
diseases such as diabetes, leukemia, and cancer.

Georgine emphasized the fact that labor unions are
unique in their mission: the betterment of the community.
They have been instrumental in winning decent housing,
decent meals, wage increases, better health care and pen-
sion benefits, civil and equal rights, and paid vacations.
In short, Georgine stated: "Unions have been the vehicle
by which many Americans have fulfilled the promise of
this great nation." Though the economy and various social
and cultural elements may threaten to undermine the social structure, he is convinced that the only way to affect
and defeat the negative forces is to take practical, decisive, concerted action and build or rebuild our communities "on the strong foundation of family, friends, religion,
and union solidarity."

Alexander Fortunatus Giacco

This highly successful chemical engineer and business executive was born in San Giovanni di Gerace, Italy, August 24, 1919, to Salvatore and Maria Concetta de Maria Giacco. When Alexander was still very young, his family emigrated to the United States and settled in Meriden, Connecticut. After attending and graduating from the elementary and the high school of that town, he matriculated for his B.S. degree at the Virginia Polytechnic Institute in Blacksburg, Virginia.

Soon after, Giacco launched on his career as an engineer with Hercules Incorporated in Wilmington, Delaware, and for the next forty-five years held a variety of increasingly responsible management positions in the research, production, marketing, planning, and international divisions of that company.

After serving as a member of the Board of Directors of Hercules (1971), he advanced to the capacity of General Manager of Hercules Europe and subsequently, to the office of Vice President, Executive Vice President, CEO and finally President. He served as Chairman of the Board from 1980 to 1987.

While still at Hercules and through December 1991, he had been on the Board of Directors and CEO both at Montedison, S.p.A. (Milan, Italy) and at Himont, Inc. (Wilmington, Delaware, and Palm Beach, Florida), as well as on the Board of Ferruzzi Finanziaria, the parent company of Montedison. He is now a Managing Partner with Axess Corporation (West Palm Beach, Florida).

Giacco's talents and achievements in his field have been recognized widely. He received honorary degrees in Law from the Catholic University of America, Washington, D.C. (1990); in Business from William Carey College, Hattiesburg, Mississippi; in Humane Letters from Mount Saint Mary's College, Emmitsburg, Maryland.

Financial World named Giacco "One of Ten Outstanding Chief Executive Officers in United States History"

(1980 and 1987). And in 1984, the same publication named him "The Best Chief Executive Officer in the Chemical Industry." Yet another publication, *The Wall Street Transcript*, honored Giacco for each year from 1983 to 1986, designating him as the "Best Chief Executive in the Diversified Chemicals Industry."

His achievements and activities, however, have not been acknowledged in industrial and academic circles alone, nor in this country exclusively. Catholic Charities, the Boys Scouts of America and the Lions International Club in Reggio Calabria, Italy, have honored him for his citizenship and achievements. The United States Government has similarly recognized his dedication and expertise by appointing him to the Advisory Council on Japan-United States Economic Relations and to the President's Private Sector Survey on Cost Control in the Federal Government.

The wealth and excellence of his contributions, both within and beyond the scope of his professional ambit, demonstrate not only his rare capabilities but also his incredible dedication and inexhaustible energy. He, himself, admits to being a "workaholic" but firmly contends that his obligations to his family have always come first ... a throwback to his Italian heritage.

"If you are fortunate to have a family," he explains, "it is a constant renewal of your years in your children and grandchildren: a reminder of what your greatest contribution has been. A good family is a great feeling of accomplishment and something that riches cannot buy ... and you have to work hard for it."

He and his wife, Edith Brown Giacco, apparently have worked hard and successfully to provide the necessary stability for their close-knit family of five: Alexander Fortunatus, Jr., Richard John, Mary Giacco Walsh, Elizabeth Giacco Brown, and Marissa Giacco Rath.

Perhaps one of the reasons why the Giaccos are still a strong unit in these days of splintered families is because of the father's position as his children grew into young adulthood: "The hardest task I had as a parent," he admits, "was to leave them alone to make their own mistakes and, more importantly, to be what they were rather than what I wanted them to be."

Finally when asked whether he had ever been the victim of prejudice as he was making his way up the corporate ladder, Alexander Giacco stated that, as a young initiate into that environment, he was frequently warned that being an Italian Catholic was an impossible barrier to any success in that world. And, indeed, there was ... and there still is ... prejudice in many guises and from many sources.

The only way to deal with prejudice, Giacco has found, is to make of it a challenge and a spur to ambitions and aspirations, rather than the deterrent and debaser it was intended to be.

References: *Directors and Executives* (1978-present)
Standard and Poor's Registry of Corporations, 1992.
Who's Who in America, 1992-1993.
Who's Who in the World, 1986.

Robert N. Giaimo

Robert N. Giaimo, former United States Representative from the Third District of Connecticut, is a Democrat from the town of North Haven. He was born in New Haven, October 15, 1919, the son of Rose and Rosario Giaimo, a founder and first president of the Community Bank and Trust Company of New Haven.

Young Giaimo attended North Haven public schools, Hillhouse High School in New Haven, then Fordham College, and the University of Connecticut School of Law, from which he received his LL.B. degree in 1943. He was admitted to the Connecticut Bar in 1947, and practiced in the New Haven area. During World War II, he served as a commissioned officer in the U.S. Army.

Prior to his service in the U.S. Congress, Mr. Giaimo served as Chairman of the State of Connecticut Personnel Appeals Board, as a member of the Board of Education, Board of Finance and Third Selectman of the Town of North Haven. He was first elected to Congress in 1958, and then was re-elected to each succeeding Congress until 1980. From 1977 to 1981 he was Chairman of the House Committee on the Budget, established by the Congress to act as the committee with overall responsibility for the federal budget. As a member of the House Committee on Appropriations since 1963, he served on the important Subcommittee on Defense with jurisdiction over the budget of the Department of Defense.

Congressman Giaimo and Senator Henry Bellmon (retired) of Oklahoma, formed and served as Co-Chairmen of the Committee for a Responsible Federal Budget, a bipartisan committee dedicated to preserving and strengthening the budget process whereby the Congress adopts and lives within budgetary restraints. Mr. Giaimo served as Co-Chairman with former Congressman John Rhodes of Arizona who succeeded Senator Bellmon.

After twenty-two years of service in the United States House of Representatives, Congressman Giaimo voluntarily retired from elected public office and did not seek re-election in 1980.

Mr. Giaimo is married to Marion Schuenemann, of Windsor, Connecticut, and their daughter, Barbara Lee Phillips, resides in Virginia. Mr. Giaimo is a member of various fraternal, civic, and veterans' organizations and served as honorary member of the Board of Gaylord Hospital, Wallingford, Connecticut, the Quinnipiac Council, Boy Scouts of America (New Haven, Connecticut). He also served as a member of the Board of Trustees of the University of New Haven.

References: *Who's Who in American Government,* 1987.
Who's Who in America, 1980-1981.

A. Bartlett Giamatti

Scholar, educator, college president, and baseball commissioner—such was the gamut of professions and careers brilliantly practiced by Angelo Bartlett Giamatti in the course of an all-too-brief life span of fifty-one years. The broad and variegated scope of his interests and pursuits might be explained, in part, by his heritage.

One grandfather was Angelo Giamattei (the original surname): he landed at Ellis Island about 1900 and settled in New Haven where he found employment as a laborer. At about the same period, the other grandfather—Bartlett Walton—was leaving Andover for Harvard College.

When Valentine Giamatti, A. Bartlett's father, entered first grade, he spoke no English. Yet as a high school graduate he won a four-year scholarship to Yale and subsequently earned a Ph.D. from Harvard. During a period of study in Florence, Italy, Valentine Giamatti met Mary Clayburgh Walton, a Smith College junior studying abroad. After her graduation they were married.

"Bart" and his sister Elvira, the children of this union, grew up in South Hadley, Massachusetts, a few blocks from Mount Holyoke College where Professor Giamatti was teaching Italian. When Bart was nine, the Giamatti family spent a year in Rome during his father's sabbatical and another year in Italy when Bart was sixteen. In later years he was to credit those years abroad for imparting to him an Italian fatalism, a sense of history, and a concern for the fragility of institutions.

Young Giamatti attended Phillips Academy in Andover, Massachusetts, and resumed rooting for the Red Sox baseball team whose progress he had enthusiastically followed from childhood. "That was the universe," he would philosophize later, "that was the firmament. What the Lord had put out there to give stability, coherence, and purpose in life." The passion for baseball apparently enhanced his passion for learning and culture. He graduated from Yale

College *magna cum laude* in 1960 and, just four years later, was awarded the Ph.D. in comparative literature from Yale University. Bartlett Giamatti joined the Yale faculty as assistant Professor of English in 1966 and advanced rapidly up the academic ranks until, at thirty-three, he attained a full professorship in English and comparative literature.

Professor Giamatti never lost sight of the student in the process of teaching the course. He devoted much time and unlimited energy to student interests, concerns, and potential. He paid special attention to planning Yale's freshman-English curriculum to ensure the students' maximum interest and involvement from the very beginning. Despite his conservatism on educational matters, his stance against pass-fail courses and his reputation as a tough marker, the students, particularly the more serious ones, responded enthusiastically to Giamatti's approach and high standards. His teaching was complemented and enriched by the study and research he continued to do on classical, medieval, and Renaissance literature. The many years of teaching, research, and writing were quite probably the halcyon days of Professor Giamatti's tenure at Yale.

As economic conditions deteriorated in the 1970's, even such prestigious universities as Yale began to experience serious financial problems. When its president, Kingman Brewster, resigned in May 1976, to become ambassador to Great Britain, the search for a new president proved frustrating. The post was offered to Professor Giamatti who accepted and became Yale's 19th president, effective July 1, 1978.

Thus, at thirty-eight, Bartlett Giamatti was the youngest Yale president in two hundred years. He was also the first of its presidents not entirely of Anglo-Saxon heritage. In an article in *The New York Times* (March 6, 1983), reporter William E. Geist remarked: "Some Old Blues felt that the choice of a Renaissance literature professor in a Boston Red Sox cap as replacement for the stately Kingman Brewster, who had abjured to become the United States Ambassador to the Court of St. James, while perhaps quaint, was certainly ill-advised."

On the other side of the coin were Professor Giamatti's positive qualifications for the position: he was a respected scholar who understood education and he had the support and the admiration of most of the faculty, and the students alike. As he himself predicted, "I'm going to hate some of the things I'll have to do, and people are going to hate me. ... I've learned from watching the academic world ... that the president persuades, or tries to persuade, the faculty. He doesn't command or issue fiats."

And persuade he obviously did, for although he hired Jerald L. Stevens to be vice president for finance and administration so that he himself could devote most of his efforts to academic matters, Giamatti's own aggressive approach to fund-raising elicited unprecedented contributions from alumni, corporations, and foundations. He traveled the country promoting a $370-million fund-raising campaign—a goal that would be exceeded by more than three-million during his tenure. Within two years, Yale university boasted its first balanced budget in a decade.

Giamatti did not neglect academic matters—the grading system, the curriculum, the proper place of athletics at Yale, necessary cuts in teaching and white-collar personnel, and cuts in their salaries, and similar problems with the blue-collar workers on campus. He staunchly maintained that the goal of Yale University traditionally had been and should continue to be liberal education. Because of his expertise, his charisma, and his proven dedication to learning and research, Giamatti was invited to speak by hundreds of groups within the United States and abroad.

Seven years at Yale took their toll on him physically. Medical tests would definitely show that during the unrest and strikes on campus, Giamatti had suffered a mild heart attack. In February 1985, after the Yale disputes had been resolved, Giamatti announced his resignation, to be effective in June 1986. He was approached by the search committee for the new president of the National League and was chosen unanimously. Peter O'Malley of the Los Angeles Dodgers, explained: "Many people say they love baseball ... but Bart has respect as well as love."

Ever the idealist, Giamatti hoped to purify the game of baseball, to clean up the national pastime. He targeted those players whose use of drugs and foul language and involvement with sex scandals and bizarre off-the-field behavior were seriously undermining the sport. Club owners, players and public alike appreciated and admired him.

In January 1989, Giamatti was chosen Commissioner of Baseball—the consummation of his childhood dream.

In a press conference, after he had announced that Pete Rose, accused of gambling and betting on baseball games, was banished forever from the game, Commissioner Giamatti stated: "I will be told that I am an idealist ... I hope so." Emotionally and physically drained from the unsavory case, he sought relaxation and renewal at his Edgartown cottage on Martha's Vineyard. The change of pace, the leisurely walks to the beach, the sorely missed family activities he had envisioned were not to be. On September 1, 1989, seven days after his final confrontation with Pete Rose, Giamatti died of a heart attack.

The untimely death of this "Renaissance Man," teacher and scholar, Ivy-League President, Baseball Commissioner, and wonderful human being was shocking and devastating. Baseball Hall of Famers and Nobel Laureates joined luminaries of the music and entertainment world to honor A. Bartlett Giamatti at a memorial in New York's Carnegie Hall. Most of the speakers, including his son, Marcus Giamatti, simply read stirring, evocative passages from his writings, such as one from his last book, *Take Time For Paradise* (Summit Books), voicing his undying conviction, "To know Baseball is to aspire to the condition of freedom."

Regarding assimilation, A. Bartlett Giamatti stated that it is "a two-way process, of giving and receiving, of becoming American while adding to America what is enduring in the energy, history and devotion to life in being

Italian. If assimilation is this reciprocity of response, as I believe it to be, then Americans of Italian heritage have much to be proud of and have millions of successes to celebrate." (See Giamatti's "Commentary," in *The Italian Americans*, by Allon Schoener.)

A member of the NIAF's International Board of Advisers, Giamatti contributed a fresh voice to the debate over higher education in America. He stressed that the university's greatest strength is its pluralism, its lack of a narrow academic mission other than the search for truth. "The university serves the country best," he writes in *A Free and Ordered Space: The Real World of the University,* "when it is a caldron of competing ideas, and not a neatly arranged platter of received opinions." Although Giamatti clearly was dismayed by growing anti-intellectualism in America, in this book he rises above his concern with one of the most eloquent defenses of the mind's nobility to come our way in a long time.

References: *Current Biography,* 1978.
A. Bartlett Giamatti, *A Free and Ordered Space: The Real World of the University,* W. W. Norton, 1988.
James Reston, Jr. *Collision at Home Plate,* July 1991.
Allon Schoener, "Commentary," in *The Italian Americans,* 1987.
The New York Times, March 6, 1983, April 28, 1985, September 5-6, 1989, December 12, 1989.

Margaret J. Giannini

Dr. Margaret J. Giannini was the recipient of the National Italian American Foundation Award in 1980, which honored her outstanding work and research in the field of medicine and for the treatment of the handicapped.

However, her initial specialty, after graduating from Hahnemann Medical College (1945) was in pediatrics. As Associate Professor in the New York Medical College (1948-67) and full Professor of Pediatrics from 1967 on, she began to concentrate on the problems of mentally retarded and physically handicapped children.

This soon led to Dr. Giannini's Mental Retardation Institute which she founded and started directing in 1950. Beginning as a clinic in Spanish Harlem, it was the first and, since then, has become the largest facility for the handicapped in the world. It was President Jimmy Carter who nominated Dr. Giannini as the Director of the National Institute on Handicapped Research in the Department of Health, Education, and Welfare. As Director, Dr. Giannini was charged with the responsibility of coordinating the many facets of research on the handicapped undertaken by the various Federal agencies.

Dr. Giannini's invaluable contribution to the project has been widely recognized; she has been made chairman of the International Seminar on Mental Retardation, and of the Mental Retardation Task Force State-Wide which plans Vocational Rehabilitation Services for the New York State Department of Education Services.

Thus Dr. Giannini's original focus on handicapped children was extended to adults, veterans or otherwise, and to mental as well as physically handicapped. Her work has impressively advanced, motivated, and inspired progress

in the field of rehabilitation through the agencies and
through her articles and speeches.

References: Biographical Index, 1980.
            Downs, F., American Legion Magazine, "Prosthetics for
            Veterans," February 1989.

Rose Basile Green

Rose Basile Green, Ph.D., has had a long, distinguished career as writer, scholar, poet, professor, and educational administrator. Although academically her area of specialization is in American and English civilization and literature, her expertise and range of interest extend far beyond that. Her pride and interest in her ethnic origins are reflected in her creative writing, in her research, and in her eclectic organizational activities.

She credits her paternal grandfather, Giovanni Basile, for the courage and foresight to have emigrated with his family from Calitri, Avellino, Italy, to the United States "in order to expand his visions of free enterprise." Her father, Salvatore, and her mother, Carolina Galgano Basile, prospered in New Rochelle, New York, as a result of their three successful business enterprises.

In time, however, they had to move to Connecticut because of Salvatore's illness. They bought a large farm in Harwinton where Rose and her siblings attended a one-room schoolhouse opposite their home, on property that Salvatore had donated to the town. The family's resourcefulness and fighting spirit of survival served as inspiration and motivation in Dr. Green's career and in her achievements.

That career began soon after she earned her B.A. degree *cum laude* from the College of New Rochelle in 1935, when Rose Basile worked for one year in Torrington, Connecticut, with the WPA's Writers' Project. Subsequently, she taught English and Italian for six years in the Torrington High School and Dramatics in the Evening Adult program of that same school.

Her interest has always been to encourage recognition of the contribution of Italian-Americans. In her prose and in her poetry there is a recurring note, lauding them for enriching the American way of life with the building trades, farming, commerce, industry, education, and other phases of American life. She has brought honor to the Italians in America as a distinguished lady in the academic and literary world.

After an interim of one year (1942-1943) as Registrar and Associate Professor of English at the University of Tampa in Florida, Dr. Green, who by then had married Raymond Silvernail Green, worked with the National Broadcasting Company in New York as a free-lance writer of radio scripts (1943-1953). The Green's two children, Carol Rae and Raymond Ferguson, were born within that decade.

Dr. Green's university-teaching career began in 1953, when she was appointed as Special Instructor of English at Temple University, and culminated with her many years (1957-1970) at Cabrini College in Radnor, Pennsylvania. Here, as one of its founders, she was an Associate Professor of English and advanced to Chairman of that Department, which also entailed her teaching courses in Modern American and British Literature. Her major scholarly work is *The Italian American Novel: A Document of Interaction of Two Cultures.* In this book, she examines seventy writers of Italian descent and demonstrates their importance, both for their aesthetic value and the social implications, critically evaluating them within the framework of American literature.

Since her academic retirement in 1970, Dr. Green continues to write and is active in national Italian American cultural and educational affairs. She has been writing book reviews, critical volumes, poetry, pamphlets and articles, and lecturing internationally, not exclusively on literature per se, but on related topics, such as: "Ethnicity and American Studies," "The Immigrant Woman in American Literature," "Italian-Americans and Other Ethnics," "The Cabrinian Philosophy of Education," and countless others. Her many volumes of poetry include: *Lauding the American Dream* (1982), *Songs of Ourselves* (1982), *The Pennsylvania People* (1984), and *Challenger Countdown* (1988). Among other works are: *Sonnets for the Constitution, Day-By-Day,* and *Five Hundred Years of America.*

Her literary and research production alone, however extensive, does not epitomize Dr. Green's activities and interests since her retirement from Cabrini College. She has been active in numerous and varied organizations, including the National Italian American Foundation (as Vice President of its first Board of Directors), the National Advisory Council of Ethnic Heritage Studies (United States Department of Education), the American Academy of Political and Social Science, the American-Italian Historical Association, the Academy of American Poets, the Academy of Vocal Arts, the Opera Company of Philadelphia, the Center for the Study of the Presidency. In many cases she has served on the Board of Directors of the organizations.

The variety and number of Dr. Green's awards attest further to her versatility and generosity and to her incredible energy and dedication. She has been granted humanitarian awards, honorary doctorates and citations by educational institutions, such as Columbia University and College of New Rochelle in New York; Cabrini and Gwynedd Colleges in Pennsylvania; and by Government and Government-related entities, such as the Republic of Italy, the City of Philadelphia, and the Daughters of the American Revolution.

Throughout her highly productive and richly rewarding careers as scholar, writer, professor and humanitarian, avowedly, she has been motivated by her "dedication and loyalty to her ancestry and by her search for truth"; therein lies her "incentive to poetize the ideals of all the people of the nation ... in general." Dr. Green underscores her conviction that "Pressure must be exerted nationally and on the printed and visual media, to affirm the accomplishments of Americans of Italian ancestry."

Rose Basile Green was awarded a Doctorate of Humane letters "Honoris Causa" from Gwynedd-Mercy College. Acknowledging her accomplishments, the President remarked: "She is a woman who has never lost her sense of personal dignity or her esteem for the humanity of other human beings."

References: *Directory of International Biography,* 1982.
   Who's Who in America, 1992-1993.
   Who's Who Among Authors and Journalists, 1988.
   Who's Who in the World, 1986.
   Who's Who of American Women, 1990-1991.
   International Who's Who in Poetry, 1993.
   Directory of American Scholars, 1982.
   Distinguished Daughters of Pennsylvania, 1978.

Dolores Hope

Born in Saratoga, New York, Dolores DeFina Hope is the daughter of an Italian father and an Irish mother. "Both my parents were born in Saratoga," she explains, "but my Italian heritage was a very important part of my background, even though English was the language spoken in our home, and today I speak Italian only *un poco.*"

One of Dolores' fondest childhood memories is of her Italian grandfather, from a mountain town between Naples and Foggia, teaching her Irish mother how to cook his favorite Italian specialties.

"Every Sunday we would have huge family get-togethers," she recalls, "and we would serve all the marvelous Italian dishes made by my mother. I have carried on that tradition to this day, putting on Sunday dinners for our children and grandchildren, with my meatballs and spaghetti as the main attraction."

Dolores DeFina enjoyed a successful singing career at New York's Vogue Club under the name of Dolores Reade. It was during his Broadway run with the hit show *Roberta* that Bob Hope met Dolores. After a year-long courtship, they were married in Erie, Pennsylvania, in 1934.

The young English-born dancer-and-song man she married was just beginning to hit his stride on the stage, after many years as a clerk, amateur boxer, and newspaper reporter. Bob stepped up to starring roles on Broadway, as well as, in films, on radio and television.

Yet Bob Hope's five "special" Academy Awards, (between 1940 and 1965), were not for his acting but for "humanitarian action" in entertaining literally millions of Americans, particularly our American troops in Vietnam. As for Dolores Hope, her energetic and wholehearted charitable endeavors have served to elevate and improve the lives of others.

Over a period of more than sixty years, Bob Hope became a household word—America's most beloved comedian; a man who commanded the nation's affection and gratitude. His renowned tours of U.S. bases began in 1931; his Christmas tours to troops stationed at military installations around the world, in 1948. Indeed, to this day, he still entertains servicemen and women with mini-tours of military and veterans' hospitals across the United States and throughout the world. On many of these tours Dolores accompanies her husband. Theirs is a union that boasts not only a durability seldom seen in show-business circles, but also a vibrant partnership based on admiration, respect, and love of family.

Since becoming Mrs. Bob Hope, Dolores has devoted herself to the raising of their four adopted children and to her widespread charitable interests. She has distinguished herself as a dynamic philanthropist through her service as President and, subsequently, as Chairman of the Eisenhower Medical Center in Palm Desert, California. She guided the large and magnificently equipped and staffed Center through its early stages and is responsible for raising millions on its behalf. In addition to her Eisenhower Medical Center activities, Mrs. Hope served also on the Board of Directors of Mutual of Omaha, United of Omaha, and the Kennedy Center of the Performing Arts in Washington.

In 1978 she and Bob were Grand Marshals for the New York Columbus Day Parade. Her subsequent activities have been too numerous to list. Dolores Hope has also been cited on many occasions. She has four honorary degrees from: St. Michael's College, St. Bonaventure University, Benedictine College, St. Louis University. She was honored as "Outstanding Catholic Laywoman" by St. Louis University and "Outstanding Mother of the Year" by Cedars-Sinai Hospital in Los Angeles.

Dolores Hope was the Honorary Mayor of Palm Springs five times and was named "Woman of the Year" by the *Los Angeles Times* in 1971. Among other distinctions, she was honored as "Chicago Lady of the Year" by Notre Dame University and received the "Eleanor Darnell Carroll" Award, from Georgetown University.

Separately, Dolores and Bob are extraordinary human beings. Together, they are an unbeatable combination. When the National Italian American Foundation honored Dolores Hope in 1986 for her extraordinary contributions, she expressed her love for Italy and its cultural heritage. Gratefully and proudly, she stated: "I thank my Italian background for whatever artistic inclinations I have. My father's forebears in Italy were all musicians and artists, so I feel certain that's where my musical talents came from."

References: *NIAF Washington Newsletter,* October 1986.

Lee Anthony Iacocca

Corporation executive, modern captain of industry, marketing genius—not commonly applied epithets for Americans born of humble immigrants! Yet they do aptly characterize Lee Iacocca and his parents, Nicola and Antoinette Perrotto Iacocca of San Marco, about twenty-five miles northeast of Naples in the Italian province of Campania.

Nicola initially came to the United States in 1902, when he was twelve years old. One long day's work in a Pennsylvania coal mine and a subsequent apprenticeship as a shoemaker set the young boy's goal in his new country—to be his own boss. Nineteen years later, he went to Italy for his widowed mother, and brought back a seventeen-year-old bride from his native town. By the time Delma, their first child, was born Nicola had opened a hot-dog restaurant which stayed afloat throughout the Great Depression. Not content with just a single venture, the dynamic Nicola bought into one of the very first car-rental agencies, building up a fleet of thirty autos—most of them Fords. Finally he hit his stride in the real estate business, investing in a few movie theaters. All these enterprises made him a millionaire, but with the Depression, Nicola lost all his money and nearly lost his house as well.

Although there were now two young mouths to feed—their son Lido (Lee) having been born in Allentown, Pennsylvania, on October 15, 1924—the resourceful parents coped effectively with the economic reversals. In the worst periods, Lee's mother went to work, either in her husband's restaurant or in a silk mill, sewing shirts. Whatever it took to keep going, she did energetically and gladly. The children, who had savored luxury for a few years, adjusted well to their reduced circumstances, thus easing their parents' burden and tensions. By the time Lee had finished ninth grade at the Stevens School, he had distinguished himself not only for his scholarship but also for leadership, having been elected president of the seventh and eighth grades and school president during the ninth grade.

He continued to excel in his studies in Allentown High School and was involved with sports and athletics when he came down with a severe case of rheumatic fever. Nevertheless, he was able to channel his competitive energies into excelling scholastically and even making the honor roll. He turned to chess, bridge, debating and, in his senior year, he was elected president of his class and a member of the National Honor Society. In retrospect he says: "The most important thing I learned in school was how to communicate."

Soon after graduation he tried to enlist in the Army since World War II had already begun, but was classified 4F because of the residual impairments from the bout with rheumatic fever. He enrolled at Lehigh University and maintained an "A" average, despite the constant teasing from his dormitory mates. He shrugged it off and explained confidentially: "I'm going to be vice president at Ford's before I'm 35." Although he wrote for the campus paper and served as its layout editor, he never neglected his studies; in fact, in only three years, he earned his B.S. degree in Industrial Engineering (1945).

After graduation, Iacocca was indeed hired by Ford Motors and sent to Dearborn, Michigan, as an executive trainee. However, before completing the 18-month program, he requested and was granted a leave of absence to accept a Wallace Memorial Fellowship for a Master of Arts degree (1946) in Mechanical Engineering at Princeton.

He returned to Dearborn to resume the training program and, in nine months, accomplished what his fellow-trainees achieved in a year and a half. He then realized that the engineering aspect of the work was too solitary, too confining and demanding. He decided to explore the sales field. While gaining invaluable experience doing everything from tending blast furnaces to tightening screws on the assembly line, he honed his communicative skills with a Dale Carnegie course and persisted in his determination to change direction.

The opportunity finally came when he was assigned to fleet sales in Chester, Pennsylvania; three years later he was promoted to zone manager in Wilkes-Barre. By 1953 he was assistant sales manager of the Philadelphia district. In 1956, he launched a sales campaign with the slogan "56 for 56," urging customers to buy Fords that year by paying $56 a month over three years. This district became number one in national Ford sales and, when the campaign was extended nationwide, it resulted in the sale of an additional 75,000 cars.

As sales proliferated, Iacocca's career soared and opportunities for advancement overlapped. Thus, just as he was settling into a new position as manager of the Washington, D.C., sales office, he was summoned to Dearborn, Michigan, to direct the national truck-marketing strategy. It was a weighty decision which meant that he and his recent bride, Mary McCleary, had to move out of the home they had just moved into. But the future was to prove his decision a sound one for, within a year, Iacocca was transferred from truck to car marketing. Soon he was put in charge of both. After his thirty-sixth birthday, he succeeded Robert McNamara as vice president and general manager of the biggest division in Ford Motors, then the world's second largest company. By just one year, he had missed fulfilling his college ambition of landing a vice presidency at age thirty-five.

The next five years were the most rewarding and exciting of Iacocca's life: challenges to be met and new ideas to be explored were shared by those he chose to work with him. "We saw ourselves as artists," he remembers, "about to produce the finest masterpieces the world had ever seen." And with a flair for marketing, for understanding and even predicting what the buying public wanted and needed, Iacocca made his first coup with the Mustang—the first auto to embody his ideas and one of the most successful cars in Detroit history. He had concentrated on a car that would appeal especially to the rapidly growing youth market and would answer the requirements of young customers: great styling, strong performance and affordable price—basically, the poor man's Thunderbird.

In 1964, it was an instant success, setting a postwar sales record in the first year alone. As the "Father of the Mustang," Iacocca continued his ascendancy in the corporate ranks. He revitalized production by introducing the sporty Mercury Cougar, and the luxurious Mercury Marquis and Lincoln Mark III.

When Henry Ford II named him President of the Corporation in 1970, Iacocca set about instituting programs designed to cut costs and streamline operations. Moreover, he continued introducing new cars, among them the Pinto and the Fiesta, both of which were money-makers, initially. Later, the Pinto turned into a disaster. Why? Gasoline prices were escalating and the federal government began imposing anti-pollution and safety standards. But worst of all, relations with Henry Ford 2nd began to deteriorate dramatically until, finally, in July of 1978, Iacocca was summarily dismissed with three months' notice.

Three days later, Iacocca took over the financially ailing Chrysler Corporation. In his capacity as President and Chief Executive Officer, he restored the company to financial health by 1983. In addition, a series of TV commercials with Iacocca as spokesman made him a media celebrity while he helped restore Chrysler's credibility. He was given the same salary with a bonus of $1.5 million to compensate for the severance pay he would forfeit from Ford.

Iacocca took on the herculean task of rescuing Chrysler from certain bankruptcy. He enforced some difficult measures: layoffs, production cutbacks and wage concessions. Most significant of all, he marshalled support from labor, management and suppliers to secure a $1.2 billion dollar loan guaranteed by the federal government. He was able to pay back the loan in full, years before it fell due, and

Chrysler was restored to financial stability. Since then, Iacocca has concentrated on introducing new models, including the K-car series and the top-selling minivan. Chrysler products were soon competing effectively with foreign automakers and the foreign market expanded considerably.

As chief executive officer of the diversified conglomerate, Iacocca states in his autobiography: "I like hands-on responsibility. If it works, give me the credit. If it doesn't, I'll take the rap." In all his endeavors, he is totally committed. He proudly served as Chairman of the Statue of Liberty-Ellis Island Centennial Commission and saw the project as a tribute not only to his own immigrant parents but also to the other seventeen-million who braved adversities to pursue a dream in America. He generously supports the Joslin Diabetes Center in Boston and is active in a wide range of charitable and civic organizations. His honorary degrees and awards are numerous, impressive and hard-earned.

Particularly after his beloved wife Mary died in 1983, Iacocca has become even more closely bonded to his daughters Kathi and Lia and their families. For, as he, himself, admitted in his autobiography, "Yes, I've had a wonderful and successful career. But next to my family, it really hasn't mattered at all."

Iacocca remains a dynamic, outspoken and persuasive spokesman for the ideals he has strongly believed in and honored all his life: equal opportunity for all Americans, pride in one's heritage and perpetuation of its culture, and a concerted improvement in American education. In a recent speech he said: "Educational standards should be raised, not lowered, if we are to survive, compete and prosper as a nation."

References: *Current Biography,* 1988.
Lee Iacocca with William Novak, *Iacocca, an Autobiography,* Bantam Books, 1984.
The New York Times, January 29, 1992.

Sophia Loren

Sophia Loren, still strikingly beautiful, slender and exotic, is not frequently seen on the American movie screen for, as in many other cases, Hollywood has few roles for actresses over fifty, glamorous though they may be.

Her life began September 20, 1934, in the charity ward for unmarried mothers of the Clinica Regina Margherita in Rome. Her mother, Romilda Villani, was a beautiful, talented but frustrated actress and pianist from the little seaport town of Pozzuoli, near Naples. Although she had won a Greta Garbo look-alike contest, her parents had forced her to forego the prize. Rebelliously, Romilda went back to Rome to try to get into the movies. Instead, she met Riccardo Scicolone, an engineering student, who charmed her but refused to marry her, even after she became pregnant.

Since the infant was in precarious health, Romilda chose to brave the consequences, return to Pozzuoli as an unwed mother, and join her parents and relatives in their already overcrowded quarters in the waterfront slum. World War 11 soon worsened the problems of living and survival. Naples, with its harbor and railroad stations, was being bombed five times a night. Sophia Loren has said about this period: "I looked death in the face every day. I was brought up with hunger and fear."

It was no surprise that Sophia was underfed and scrawny, even into her early teens in post-war Pozzuoli. In fact, she was nicknamed "stecchetto" (little stick) and "stuzzicadenti" (toothpick). However, she must have caught up by the time she was fourteen, for at that age she entered the first of several beauty contests in Naples and won the title of "Princess of the Sea."

This was enough to prompt her mother to try her luck (and also her daughter's) in Cinecittà —the movie-making center on the outskirts of Rome. They both won parts as extras in *Quo Vadis,* but did not qualify for even one-or-two-line speaking roles because they didn't know English. From then on Sophia, at least, concentrated on becoming multilingual. She went on to win the Miss Italy Beauty Contest, being dubbed "Miss Elegance." Her mother became discouraged and decided to concentrate only on her daughter's career instead of her own.

When movie jobs were scarce and beauty contests no longer imminent, Sophia turned to modeling for "fumetti," the illustrated pulp novels and comic strips which had the dialogue in balloons. She managed to earn a modest living from these triple endeavors, but her real break came when the Miss Rome Beauty Contest attracted a certain Dr. Carlo Ponti, a balding Milanese lawyer, as one of the judges. He signed her to a contract, sent her to drama coaches and put her in films, first as Sofia Lazzaro and then later, in more important roles, as Sophia Loren.

By 1954, she was an established star in Italy and began vying with Gina Lollobrigida for choice movie roles to capture the attention of moviegoers overseas as well. Tall, statuesque, and sensuous of face and form, she honed her comedic and dramatic talents in her own country, especially in films which combined her talents with those of Vittorio de Sica and Marcello Mastroianni *(The Miller's Beautiful Wife, The Sign of Venus,* etc.). She was soon flooded with offers from Hollywood producers. Her first role in an American movie was *The Pride and the Passion,* co-starring Cary Grant and Frank Sinatra.

Less than a year later, in 1958, Sophia Loren went to Hollywood to co-star with Cary Grant in *Houseboat.* This was a signal period for her career as well as for her personal fortunes, since Carlo Ponti had been courting her, despite the fact that he was married, though separated. Hollywood's frenetic publicity campaign heralding her as the new sex goddess and Cary Grant's interest in his seductive co-star might have intensified Mr. Ponti's efforts. He arranged a quick Mexican divorce, by proxy, and he and Sophia Loren were speedily married.

Hollywood provided an extraordinary learning experience as she worked with outstanding directors and actors. Throughout her career she has had similar positive experiences in Italy, England and France.

By 1961, Miss Loren was back in Italy, where she gave the most memorable performance of her career in de Sica's *La Ciociara* (Two Women). Her powerful, tragic portrayal of a single mother in war-ravaged Italy won her the first Academy Award for Best Actress ever given to a foreign star in a foreign-language film. The same film also won her the Cannes Festival Award and many other coveted international citations. Her flair for comedy was recognized when she earned Best Actress nominations for *Yesterday, Today and Tomorrow* and *Marriage Italian Style.* Both of these had the familiar magic ingredients—Marcello

Mastroianni as co-star, and Vittorio de Sica as director. *Marriage Italian Style* also won the Moscow Festival Acting Award. All her American-sponsored films since 1960 have been made abroad.

As recently as 1989, Sophia Loren faced one of her greatest professional challenges—in Carlo Ponti's European remake of *Two Women* which had won her an Academy Award in 1961. In a tour de force unique in film industry history, she played her original role as the twenty-five-year-old mother of a fifteen-year-old daughter, but she played it with the broadened informed insight of an actress who had herself experienced motherhood.

In her latest film, *Saturday, Sunday and Monday,* directed by Lina Wertmuller, she plays the mother in the saga of a large, noisy, and eccentric Neapolitan family. As might be expected, it was filmed in Pozzuoli, Miss Loren's native village. One can only imagine the emotional impact this must have had on the profoundly sensitive, fiercely loyal, waif-turned-millionairess movie star.

In 1991, the Academy of Motion Picture Art and Sciences crowned her acting career with an honorary Oscar for her outstanding contribution to films. Although her career has included more than eighty pictures, co-starring Hollywood's most sought-after leading men, Sophia Loren can indeed be proud of many other achievements.

Her marriage to Carlo Ponti has brought her the love and stabilizing security she needed, including residences in Paris, Rome, Geneva, Tuscany, Florida, California and

New York. Both the real estate holdings and her art collection are rumored to be worth several billion dollars.

More precious to the Ponti's than their material wealth are their two sons, Carlo, Jr., and Edoardo. The older son, now twenty-four, is a serious, introspective music student who plays piano, practices three hours a day and aspires to become a conductor. Edoardo, twenty, is outgoing, brimming with charm and humor, and hopes to follow his mother into the movie business, not only as an actor (he has already starred with her in one film), but also as a director.

In April 1989, Miss Loren headed an AIDS benefit on Williams Island, Florida, to raise money to fight what she describes as the "plague of the century."

In 1991, Sophia Loren was chosen as the first female grand marshal of the famous Columbus Day Parade in New York City. Another unique honor was from the United Nations Food and Agriculture Organization which chose to put her on a commemorative coin marking its twentieth year. She was represented as Ceres, the Roman goddess of grain and harvests—no mean crown for a confirmed Earth Mother and motion-picture Venus.

References: Christopher Anderson, *Ladies Home Journal,* "Viva Sophia!" April 1990.

Cawkwell and Smith, *The World Encyclopedia of the Film,* Galahad Books, New York, 1972.

A.E. Hotchener, *Sophia, Living and Loving,* William Morrow and Co., New York, 1979.

Ephraim Katz, *The Film Encyclopedia,* Putnam Publishing, 1982.

People Weekly, "Sophia Loren," July 6, 1991.

Marlene Fanta Shyer, *McCalls,* "Sophia, the Private Woman," May 1989.

Henry Mancini

Henry Mancini, the multi-talented, highly successful musician, performer and arranger, owes his early exposure to music to his Italian immigrant parents, particularly to his determined father. Born April 16, 1924, in Cleveland, Ohio, to Quinto and Anna Pece Mancini, Henry was only five years old when the family moved to West Aliquippa, Pennsylvania, where his father was hired to work in the steel mills.

Quinto Mancini, a native of Abruzzi, Italy, was unlike most of his compatriots—he definitely did not want his son to be doomed to work in the steel mills. He dreamed of a brighter future for him instead, and worked all the harder to provide for him a solid academic education, enriched by a sound musical training from early childhood.

He began by teaching his son the piccolo when he was eight years old. Henry, however, switched to the flute and then, at age twelve, to the piano. Initially, the boy found practicing distasteful and, much to his father's annoyance, seemed to prefer football. All that changed abruptly and definitively when he discovered jazz. Then he enthusiastically joined the school band and soon was made first flutist in the Pennsylvania All-State High School Band.

Henry was barely fourteen when he was accepted into the Ambridge Community Band and the Sons of Italy Band of which his father was a member. That same year he played piano with the Mel Koehler Orchestra in Beaver Falls, Pennsylvania, and played many gigs with other orchestras and bands as the occasion arose.

Although he had formal training on the flute and piano, young Henry started arranging on his own when he was fourteen. Once again his father recognized the importance of training in that discipline, and arranged for Henry to study with Max Adkins whom Mancini now acknowledges as the most important influence of his life—his own Professor Higgins. Adkins, indeed, taught him much more beyond theories and techniques and all the intricacies of arranging music; he also schooled the young recruit in the essential social amenities and introduced him to important figures in the world of contemporary music—especially Benny Goodman.

Subsequently, the young man studied at the Carnegie Institute in Pittsburgh and at Juilliard in New York. At eighteen, he registered for the draft and thanks to the ministrations of Captain Glenn Miller, the band leader, he was assigned to the 28th Air Force Band. After serving three years at home and in Europe, he was discharged March 30, 1946. He immediately went to work as pianist and arranger for the late Glenn Miller's Band which was being reorganized by Tex Beneke.

A year later, Mancini married Ginny O'Connor, popular singer with the Mello Larks group. After the honeymoon the young couple settled in Burbank, California, strategically close to the flourishing motion-picture industry and possible jobs for both Henry and Ginny. While waiting for opportunity the ambitious young musician enhanced and honed his talents with serious study with composers Mario Castelnuovo-Tedesco, Ernst Krenek and Dr. Alfred Sendrey.

Happily the tide began to turn for the young couple in 1952, when Henry joined the composing staff of Universal-International Film Studios. For the next six years, he contributed background music and scores to more than one hundred films. The one particularly close to his heart was *The Glenn Miller Story* (1954), not only because it honored his idol but also because it won Mancini his first nomination for the coveted Academy Award.

However, his score for the television series "Peter Gunn" was the real turning point in his career because, as he himself sees it, "That use of the jazz idiom, applied dramatically to the story, put music on everybody's mind as far as T.V. is concerned." The critics largely agreed, giving him credit for having given a new impetus to music composed and recorded especially for television; they praised him for adjusting his usual style to accommodate a small combo and keying it exquisitely to enhance the dramatic action.

The music from that series also won him several Grammy Awards. The album, "More Music from Peter Gunn," has sold more than one-million copies. The score was also nominated for an Emmy by the Academy of Television Arts and Sciences as the best musical score of the year.

In 1959, in collaboration with Blake Edwards, Mancini turned his talents and efforts to yet another "private-eye" series—"Mr. Lucky." Utilizing strings and organ rather than a jazz combo, Mancini composed music that resulted in a best-selling album and two additional Grammys.

Returning to the Hollywood domain, this time as a free-lance composer, Mancini achieved off-beat effects by using and combining numerous unconventional instruments, *i.e.,* untuned pianos, calliopes, African instruments and the like. He exploited the freedom allowed him by rearranging his own music, pointing up the themes he chose and recording them under ideal conditions.

Perhaps the most haunting of such compositions is "Moon River," with lyrics by Johnny Mercer, which obsessively permeates the entire sound track of *Breakfast at Tiffany's* as it is played by an amplified harmonica. The song won two Oscars for Mancini: one for Best Song and the other for the Best Musical Score for a Dramatic or Comedy Picture. In addition, it has sold over two-million albums. The following year, Mancini became the first composer ever to win Oscars in two successive years. This time it was for the title song of the movie *Days of Wine and Roses* (1962); subsequently, he was also awarded a cluster of Grammys for all of his music in that same film. During the ensuing fifteen years, Mancini continued to enliven, embellish and punctuate numerous movies with background music, arrangements and songs. By 1977, he had accumulated twenty Grammys (more than any other single musician at that time), and to date has seventy-two Grammy nominations. He won his fourth Academy Award in 1982 for the Best Original Song Score in the extremely successful comedy film *Victor/Victoria*.

Mancini's talent sweeps the field of recorded music. Eight of his ninety and more widely varied albums have been certified "gold" by the Recording Industry Association of America. In view of his productivity, it seems incredible that Henry Mancini could find the time and energy for other activities and interests—artistic or otherwise—but he can and he does. He generally conducts fifty times a year, at home and abroad. It might be the London Symphony Orchestra, the Israeli Philharmonic, or the Boston Pops. He has appeared before the British Royal Family in several command performances in 1966, 1980 and 1984.

Futhermore, he has collaborated with or arranged joint concerts with such musical luminaries as Luciano Pavarotti and James Galway. However, he does not ignore or underestimate the young and untried; for not only is he lavish with scholarships offered to aspiring and deserving young composers, musicians and artists, but he has also written two books to guide and advise them: *Sounds and Scores* and *A Practical Guide to Professional Orchestration*. With his most recent book, *Did They Mention the Music?*, Mancini offers a broad-stroked composite of himself, his family, friends, and associates and of his multifaceted life.

Published in 1989, the book is dedicated to his wife of forty-five years with the avowal that "the journey could not have been made without our love for each other." Ginny, Henry and their children—son, Chris, and twin daughters, Felice and Monica—grow closer with the years. When asked how tall he is—probably since he does not fit the stereotyped concept of the Italian male—he handsome, urbane Mancini answered: "Six-one. And six-two when

I've got a hit!" He has come a long way but he has never forgotten his roots and his Italian heritage.

References: *Current Biography,* H.W. Wilson Co., 1964.
David Ewen, *All the Years of American Pop Music,* Prentice-Hall, 1977.
Henry Mancini (with Gene Lees), *Did They Mention the Music?* Contemporary Books, 1989.
Who's Who in America, 1964-1965.

Margherita Marchione

Educator, scholar, writer, professor emerita, as well as college president, administrator, and treasurer of the Religious Teachers Filippini, Margherita Marchione was born on February 19, 1922, in Little Ferry, New Jersey, the youngest of eight children.

In the early 1900's her father, Crescenzo Marchione, emigrated from Pontecagnano, a small village near Salerno,

Italy. He soon sent for his wife, Felicia Schettino, who arrived with their first daughter. After several years in Bloomville, New York, where they started a dairy farm, the family settled in New Jersey.

Those were wonderful years of serenity, warm neighborly relationships and affection. But the family peace was shattered in 1935, when their youngest offspring Margherita announced with finality, that she was leaving to enter a religious community. Despite their surprise, sorrow and objections, her determination won out. It is this same undaunting spirit and resoluteness that have been Sister Margherita Marchione's unfailing characteristics throughout the years. Little did they dream that young Margherita would bring to their name a lasting resonance, and make a significant contribution to the history and culture of both America and Italy.

Margherita Marchione is unique among Italian-American women who have succeeded in their careers. For her, service is no burden; it is a treasured privilege. She is proud of her heritage, courageous, and compassionate. She has been a "liberated" member of society, as well as a wonderfully gifted member of the Religious Teachers Filippini. She has a charming personality that captivates her students and friends.

Sister Margherita Marchione's life is an inspiration. Her success is based on the conviction that one can inspire others only by example and love. Hers is a living experience as she helps people live intensely and enrich their lives. For this and for her legacy to the world, she will always be esteemed and honored both nationally and internationally.

When Marchione began her studies at Columbia University, where she obtained the M.A. (1949) and Ph.D. (1960), she did not know that Professor Giuseppe Prezzolini would help change the course of her life. Certainly she did not renounce her religious vocation, nor did her mentor ever advise her to do so. She admits, however, that all her accomplishments may be attributed to his encouragement: "Prezzolini awakened in me a great love for Italian culture and literature and, by his example of moral integrity, taught me to appreciate spiritual and human values."

That she became his protegee is evident from the recently published book, *Lettere a Suor Margherita* (1992). This book reveals a period of twenty-five years of friendship with her "professor" and is the story of his association with twentieth century Italian culture. Prezzolini not only appreciated Marchione's talents, but also admired and respected her faith and mission as a member of the Religious Teachers Filippini.

In 1960, her first book, *L'imagine tesa,* was released in Rome, Italy, by Edizioni di Storia e Letteratura, where she joined prestigious scholars—Kristeller, Leclerq, Praz, Ullman, Wilkins—and became one of its most prolific contributors. Later, an English adaptation, entitled *Clemente Rebora,* was published in Twayne's World Author Series. Her recent biography, *From the Land of the*

Etruscans, is the story of Lucy Filippini, a seventeenth
century educator. Among her thirty volumes are Clemente
Rebora's correspondence and that of his contemporary,
Giovanni Boine. She is co-editor of a collection of
Prezzolini's correspondence with many internationally
known literary and philosophical writers and leaders of
the twentieth century, such as Benedetto Croce, Giovanni
Papini, Aldo Palazzeschi.

Over this half century, Marchione has amassed a wealth
of honors and awards. Among them are the Columbia
University Garibaldi Scholar award (1957), Fulbright
Scholar (1964), AMITA award (1971), UNICO National
Rizzuto award (1977), Star of Solidarity of the Republic
of Italy (1977). She was honored in 1984 at the National
Italian American Foundation Congressional Awards Dinner in Washington, D.C., for her achievement in the field
of literature and historical research.

Freedoms Foundation at Valley Forge selected her for
the George Washington Honor Medal for excellence in
the category of Individual Achievement (1985). She received the National Italian American Bar Association "In-
spirational" award (1987); the "Toscani nel Mondo" award
and the honorary Doctor of Humane Letters degree by
Ramapo College of New Jersey (1990). She was also
included in the book, *Past and Promise, Lives of New
Jersey Women.*

In 1992, among other awards, Sister Margherita received the "Philip Mazzei-Thomas Jefferson International

Award" in Florence, Italy. Because of her contribution to the Italian-American community, she was given the "Arts Award" by the New Jersey Christopher Columbus Quincentennial Observance Commission. On the same occasion, in tribute to her leadership in the State, she also received *Resolutions* from both the New Jersey Senate and the New Jersey General Assembly. She is the recipient of a *Michael* from the New Jersey Literary Hall of Fame (1993).

Although teaching and research were part of her life and mission, Margherita Marchione's research expertise was challenged when, in 1974, Dr. Peter Sammartino, Chancellor of Fairleigh Dickinson University, asked her to investigate a little-known patriot, Philip Mazzei. With grants from the New Jersey Bicentennial Commission, National Historical Publications and Records Commission, National Endowment for the Humanities and, among other private foundations, the Henry and Grace Salvatori Foundation, she dedicated ten years to researching and writing about Mazzei's contributions to the creation of the United States. She published *Jefferson's "Zealous Whig"* (1975), Mazzei's, *My Life and Wanderings* (1980), *The Comprehensive Microform Edition of His Papers, 1730-1816, with Guide and Index,* 9 reels (1982), *Selected Writings and Correspondence,* 3 vols. (1983, English edition; 1984, Italian edition), and *The Constitutional Society of 1784* (1984). Her world-wide research resulted in the collection of 3,000 documents, now preserved at the Salvatori Center for

Mazzei Studies in Morristown, New Jersey, and at the American Philosophical Society Library in Philadelphia. Instrumental in obtaining an Italian stamp and a United States international airmail stamp in 1980 (with the words "Philip Mazzei Patriot Remembered"), Marchione herself was included as No. 144 of the Women's History Series of First Day Covers by the National Organization of Women.

Marchione's work has been the source of inspiration for *Adventurers of Freedom*—the TV miniseries soon to be produced, featuring the parallel lives of Jefferson and Mazzei. Her crusade to give Mazzei a place of prominence in the creation of our nation has been successful.

Throughout the years, Margherita Marchione has been interviewed and featured on several TV programs and has written innumerable articles and book reviews. Her own books range from historical research to a biography of the poet Rebora (1960); from a bilingual anthology, *Twentieth Century Italian Poetry* (1974), to *A Pictorial History of the St. Lucy Filippini Chapel* (1992), for the 300th anniversary of The Pontifical Institute of the Religious Teachers Filippini. For this occasion she also obtained a commemorative stamp from the Italian Government honoring the Sisters for their work in the field of education and for the impact they have on society at large, as they further the gospel values of justice and peace.

Among other activities, Marchione was editor and publisher of several books and journals through the American Institute of Italian Studies. She also served as general contractor for building projects at Villa Walsh, Morristown, New Jersey, where the Religious Teachers Filippini are located. For ten years, Sister Margherita personally directed summer sessions in Italy; initially through Fairleigh Dickinson University, and later she continued the program at Corfinio College in association with Edison State College.

Sister Margherita Marchione has been described as a whirlwind of exceptional deeds, a caring person with the kind of warm personality that immediately makes one feel she has been a friend for years. She is relentless in the pursuit of her objectives and committed to the Italian-American community. She has been called "a mixture of Catholicism and American independence" *(La Nazione,* July 28, 1957). It is this indomitable spirit of independence, dedication and tenacity that posterity will acknowledge.

Perhaps the inscription on the Christopher Columbus "Woman of the Year" award best sums up her achievements: "Sister Margherita Marchione—whose indispensable contributions as a great woman of God, educator and historian, whose scholarly life will stand forever as a symbol of the bond of sentiment between Italy and America, a molder of men and women in her exemplary life who has dictated exceptional awareness to the minds of our young leaders of tomorrow, we honor her, a true daughter of Columbus."

Her mission found its origins in God and, undauntingly, she accepted every challenge. Her confidence in Divine Providence is unshakable. Her love of action is reflected in her desire to participate in the life of the Religious Teachers Filippini where she served as treasurer for twenty years; in the affairs of the State under three governors as a member of the New Jersey Historical Commission for fifteen years; in elementary, secondary and higher education for fifty years; in many educational, cultural and religious organizations; in the world at large, for she respects each individual and assists all who approach her as she dares to become involved in their problems.

References: Joan Babbage, *The Star Ledger,* "Interfaith Studies," October 27, 1992.
Books in Print, Database, R.R.Bowker Co., 1992.
Contemporary Authors, 1984.
Piero Palumbo, *Gente,* "La scoperta di una suora italo-americana," December 5, 1980.
La Follia di New York, "Writer, Translator, Teacher," January 1983, July-August 1992.
Famiglia Cristiana, "Le ricerche di una suora," June 22, 1988.
Carlo Cantini, *Il Congresso,* "Suor Margherita Marchione," October 10, 1989.
Meg Dooley, *Columbia,* "Sister Margherita Marchione, Citizen of the World," Winter 1992.
Past and Promise, Lives of New Jersey Women. The Scarecrow Press, Inc., 1990.
Who's Who of American Women, 1989-1990.
Winerip, Michael, *The New York Times,* "A Splendid Nun...," October 23, 1990.

Dan Marino

Dan Marino, the Miami Dolphins' star quarterback, rose to National Football League superstardom faster than any signal caller before him. He is also credited with being largely responsible for shifting the emphasis in professional football from the run to the pass. Thanks to his extraordinarily strong arm, coupled with his lightning-fast release, his passing efficiency rating (according to the NFL evaluation standards), is the highest in the league's history.

His athletic bent manifested itself quite early in life. Daniel Constantine Marino, Jr., was born September 15, 1961, in Pittsburgh, Pennsylvania. The eldest of three children, and the only son of Dan and Veronica Kolczynski Marino, he grew up in a middle-class, Italian-Irish neighborhood. He attended St. Regis Catholic parochial school. Young Dan played quarterback on the school's team, which his father coached, and developed his arm by practicing with him after school. The quarterback, today, attributes his now famous fast release and sidearm throwing motion to those early lessons. However, when his scholastic performance showed signs of suffering (due to the emphasis on sports), it was again his father who urged and helped him to reshift the balance.

As a result, he not only earned admission to the high school of his choice, one of Pittsburgh's top athletic schools, but he also maintained a "B" average throughout the years. This he managed despite broadening his athletic activities as a star on the school's baseball team as well as on its football team. He compiled pitching and batting records that distinguished him as one of Pennsylvania's outstanding high school athletes, and led the Cincinnati Reds to scout him long before his graduation.

Meanwhile, the University of Pittsburgh had begun scouting him during his sophomore year, and in his junior year they actively tried to sign him for their football team.

To complicate his final decision, the Kansas City Royals offered him an opportunity to play professional baseball.

For a time, Marino was tempted to accept both offers, but ultimately decided to concentrate instead on football, at the University of Pittsburgh. Apparently the human consideration won out, for as he explained during a press conference, "I have strong personal and family ties to the city of Pittsburgh." From his freshman year on, Marino made his mark on college football. As a freshman in 1979, he led his team to five straight wins which included the defeat of Pittsburgh's arch-rival, Penn State, and a win over Arizona in the post-season Fiesta Bowl. As a sophomore, he threw for fifteen touchdowns and led the Panthers to another 11-1 record, including a victory in the Gator Bowl.

His best season, however, proved to be his junior year when he set Pittsburgh records with thirty-seven touchdown passes, 2876 passing yards, and 226 completed passes. During that same year he threw six touchdown passes against South Carolina and topped his all-American season with three touchdowns against Georgia in a 24-20 victory in the Sugar Bowl. One of these came dramatically in the final thirty-five seconds and won the game for the Pittsburgh Panthers which thus finished at 11-1 for the third straight season.

By the beginning of his senior year, Marino was recognized as the best quarterback in college football and the Panthers as a near-invincible team. Yet, although Marino passed for 2432 yards and totaled seventeen touchdown passes, the season was less than spectacular both for him and the Panthers. His previous outstanding achievements, however, so outweighed his senior-year record, that he still finished his college career as Pittsburgh's all-time, total-offense leader, with 8290 yards. Only the fourth of the college's players ever to have his uniform number retired, he set school records for career touchdown passes (79), passing yards (8597) and passes completed (693). He ranked fourth in touchdown passes, fifth in passing yardage, and fourth in completions in the history of NCAA.

Soon after earning his bachelor's degree from the University of Pittsburgh in 1983, Marino was signed to a four-year, two-million-dollar contract with the Miami Dolphins. Only three weeks into his rookie season, Marino replaced star quarterback, David Woodley, late in a game against the Los Angeles Raiders. The Dolphins lost that game, even though Marino had provided all of the team's final score. The very next week, the rookie got his first starting assignment in a game against the Buffalo Bills. Although the Dolphins lost, it was a much closer game, 38-35, and Marino's spectacular playing made the difference. The jubilant Don Shula made him the starting quarterback from then on. Moreover, the perceptive coach set about adapting the Dolphins' offense tactics to Marino's skills rather than the other way around. In fact, Marino, though only a rookie, changed strategies throughout the NFL by demon--strating that a team could win by relying largely on the pass for its offensive tactics.

Marino more than justified his coach's respect for his skill and talents during the rest of the season and subsequent years as well. From his 1983 Rookie of the Year Award and his selection as the first rookie to be selected as a starter in the Pro Bowl, he proceeded to win the NFL Most Valuable Player Award after a spectacular 1984 season, highlighted by incredible plays, forty-eight touchdowns, and feats which, according to Greg Logan of *Newsday* (January 21, 1985), "left NFL coaches and players gasping in amazement."

Over the next several years, Marino amassed an incredible array of records. This included his being the first quarterback in the history of the NFL to have four-4000-yard seasons; these were in '84, '85, '86, and '88. Even in 1986 and 1987, when the Dolphin defense faltered, Marino, himself, continued to excel, leading the conference in passing (throwing for 4746 yards, the third-highest total in NFL history), in touchdowns (44, second all-time to his own 48 in 1984), in completions (263) and touchdown passes (26).

Despite the Dolphins' poor showing in the latter years of the '80s, Marino continued to shine. In October 1988, he threw for 521 yards against the New York Jets, the second-highest one-game total in NFL history. He has been in the Pro Bowl in five of his seasons with the Dolphins and continues to amaze teammates, competitors and fans alike with spectacular rallies, such as, in the game against the Kansas City Chiefs in January of 1991.

Already with an impressive career in college and professional football, Marino is young, handsome, and with a six feet-four physique which has made him a matinee idol of sorts. Away from the limelight, however, he is a dedicated family man, married since January 30, 1985, to the former Claire Veazey, and father to their two sons, Daniel Charles, and Michael Joseph. Some reporters and teammates have characterized him as a down-to-earth, easygoing man who remains dedicated to the working-class values he was brought up with. Despite his crowded schedule, he continues to donate time to the Leukemia Fund and to posters for the American Library Association aimed at encouraging and promoting reading. He is also active in the Miami chapter of the National Italian-American Hall of Fame.

In September 1991, when Marino signed a five-year, twenty-five-million-dollar contract, making him the highest paid player in football history, he commented that only ten years earlier he had been making ten dollars an hour pouring concrete for a construction project at Pittsburgh's Three Rivers Stadium.

References: *Current Biography,* H.W. Wilson & Co.,1989.
Michael Jaffe, *Sports Illustrated,* "Signed,"
     September 2, 1991.
Peter King, *Sports Illustrated,* "Auld Lang Syne,"
     September 24, 1990.
Rick Reilly, *Sports Illustrated,* "Well, Look
     Who's Back," January 14, 1991.

Vincent Marotta

"Destiny" has certainly had a hand in changing the course of Vincent Marotta's life on more than one occasion but, each time, with hard work, grit and resourcefulness, he managed to keep his own hand firmly on the helm. As a result, not only did he survive each reversal of fortune, but actually worked it to his own advantage.

Born February 22, 1924, in Cleveland, Ohio, he was one of two sons of Charles Marotta and Josephine Mirabella who had emigrated from Italy. Charles settled in Massilon, Ohio, and later moved to Cleveland where he met and married Josephine. There he started his own coal company with trucks delivering coal from the rich mines of Ohio and Pennsylvania.

Charles Marotta was a quiet, hard-working man, happy with his life's achievements: providing a safe and sound home for his family and a better education than he had had for his sons, Vincent and Thomas. Both sons attended Shaker Heights High School and, with the help of an athletic scholarship, Vincent went on to become the first Marotta to attend college.

While a history major at Mount Union College in Alliance, Ohio, Vincent set records in track and football. His versatility was exceptional. When Marotta was a college sophomore, the St. Louis Cardinals baseball team offered him a contract and a chance to fulfill a lifelong dream—to play baseball in the Major Leagues. But "fate" stepped in—this time it was World War II—and Marotta enlisted in the service and was called to active duty only days before the start of baseball spring training.

With the end of the war, Marotta returned to Mount Union College and continued with football and track. In football, he still holds the all-time record of 7.9 yards per carry and he was selected First Team All-Ohio. He also starred in track and his most memorable feat came when he broke three track records at Kent State University on the same day. Marotta also tied the time of Harrison Dillard, Olympic sprint star, in the 100-Yard Dash with a record of 9.7 seconds. Dillard later went on to win the gold medal for the United States in the 1950 Olympics. Before long, Marotta caught the eye of the Cleveland Browns professional football team and they signed him to a contract. He stayed only briefly with the Browns, believing his greater success could be achieved in business.

Recognizing an up-turn in Post-War real estate, he turned his energy to the real estate development business, and within a few years, The Marotta-Glazer Company had succeeded in building over 5000 homes, office buildings, apartment complexes, and shopping malls. Once again, however, his well-earned success was made to yield to forces beyond his control. This time, it was the flagging national economy and a slowdown in the real estate industry. Characteristically, Marotta refused to despair and opted to change course, venturing into further uncharted waters—the world of inventing and manufacturing.

Vincent Marotta believed that in order to be successful, he had to offer people a better, faster, more convenient product. He became aware that coffee did not taste quite as good at home as it did in the restaurants. Therefore, he organized a company and set out to make a better cup of coffee for the home.

After three long years of research and development with numerous setbacks and frustrations, Marotta made the breakthrough that held the key to that better cup of coffee. He discovered that the ideal brewing temperature for coffee is 200 degrees Fahrenheit. From this basic principle emerged the world-famous "Mr. Coffee" coffee maker. Marotta's invention became a household word in America and forever changed the way Americans made coffee.

The path of Mr. Coffee's success has made marketing history. With four patents granted in the United States and still others abroad, distribution was established in major department stores and discount houses. A series of television commercials and other promotional outlets featured the American sports hero, Joe Di Maggio. From then on, "Mr. Coffee" dominated the industry and became the largest selling coffee maker in the world. Even after achieving great financial success with the company, Marotta remained the driving force in the business for more than fifteen years until retiring in 1987.

In recognition of his business achievements, Marotta has received numerous awards, including The Horatio Alger Award by Dr. Norman Vincent Peale, New York (1975); The Outstanding American Award, Cleveland, Ohio (1979); The Outstanding Italian-American Man-of-the-Year Award, Detroit, Michigan (1980); Commendatore al Merito della Repubblica Italiana, Washington, D.C. (1980); and his induction into the Football Hall of Fame, Mount Union College (1973).

Marotta currently spends time enjoying his two homes in Florida and Cleveland with his wife, Ann, six children and three grandchildren. When asked the time-worn question posed to most self-made individuals, that is, to what he ascribes his success, Marotta unhesitatingly answers: "Work, work, work at whatever you believe in; then perhaps, with the grace of God, you will make it happen. Don't let the *nay-sayers* discourage you from pursuing what your instincts tell you is right." Marotta's conversation is constantly peppered with allusions to his Italian heritage, of which he is patently proud. He fervently hopes that the distorted image some may have of Italian-Americans can be corrected. He is convinced that to counteract and deflect unfair prejudice, Italian-Americans must discipline themselves through purposeful direction and better education. "They must observe the precepts of Our Lord, love family and fellow man or woman, and set an example for others to follow."

Marotta is a brilliant exponent of Italian-American ingenuity, diligence and constructive energy. He reminds his compatriots that "it is very important to be proud of who you are and of your magnificent heritage. These are two elements that provide a richness and joy to your life that no turn of fate can damage or diminish. Stand tall and say—*Io son orgoglioso d'essere Italo-Americano!* (I am proud to be an Italian-American!)"

References: *I-AM*, New York, July 1977, Vol. 1, No. 9.
The Plain Dealer, Cleveland, April 14, 1974.

Gian Carlo Menotti

This Italian-born composer, playwright, arranger and director is acknowledged to be the most often performed living composer of opera. Providing his own librettos, he has brought to traditional opera the realism and timelessness of the contemporary theater.

Born in Cadegliano, a small town on Lake Lugano in Lombardy, on July 7, 1911, he was the sixth child of

Alfonso and Ines Pellini Menotti. The family was well-to-do, realizing a considerable income from a coffee-importing enterprise. The Menottis were a very musical family; besides having their own box at the La Scala Opera House, they also formed their own chamber group. At an early age, Gian Carlo was taught to play violin, cello and piano; he began composing music at six and had written two operas by the time he was thirteen years old.

His mother, Ines Menotti, was a woman of strong character, high ideals, and great ambition for her son. In 1928, after her husband's death, she brought Gian Carlo to the United States, bearing a letter of recommendation from Mrs. Arturo Toscanini. The boy was soon enrolled at the prestigious Curtis Institute of Music in Philadelphia, where he majored in composition under the well-known teacher, Rosario Scalero. His intensive training at Curtis would be of great significance, personally as well, since it was there he befriended Samuel Barber, who became a celebrated musician and composer and his lifelong close friend and collaborator.

After graduation and several years of teaching at the Curtis Institute, Menotti turned his efforts to composing: concertos, cantatas, a symphony and more than twenty operas, for which he wrote his own original librettos. The first of these, the one-act opera-buffa about a frivolous woman determined to go to a ball at all costs, was produced on Broadway at the Metropolitan Opera House in 1938. *Amelia Goes to the Ball* was so enthusiastically received, that NBC-Radio commissioned Menotti to write an opera for broadcasting.

Menotti accordingly wrote *The Old Maid and the Thief,* a comic opera about a love-smitten spinster who is not above framing a reluctant boarder as a criminal, to prevent him from escaping her clutches. After its initial success on radio, the opera was adapted for the stage and performed widely during World War II.

However, Menotti's first attempt at "grand opera" was not equally well received. *The Island God* (1942), though eventually produced at the Metropolitan Opera House, was not favorably accepted by the critics. Menotti attributed this totally to inadequate staging and from that time on insisted on directing his own pieces.

That decision undoubtedly contributed to the resounding success of subsequent Menotti creations, particularly the one-act curtain-raiser, *The Telephone* and its two-act companion feature, *The Medium.* In Menotti's estimate, the latter—a macabre thriller—is the basis for all his other work; in it the world of the occult and the supernatural is explored through the life of a medium who is caught between two worlds, one based on reality, the other on faith. Menotti himself feels that the recitative in that opera—the "parlar cantando" marked a step forward in enabling actors to talk and act out a story in musical terms.

Three years later, Menotti's grim, political, three-act tragedy, *The Consul,* enjoyed a successful run on Broadway and won the composer his first Pulitzer Prize in music. Along with *The Medium,* it continues to enjoy great popularity and has been given hundreds of performances in the major opera houses of the world, where they are considered classics.

However, Menotti's next successful creation was quite different in theme and form from his previous efforts. It was *Amahl and the Night Visitors,* a one-act opera, and the first expressly intended for television. It is the story of a crippled boy who is miraculously cured of his handicap after he offers his crutches to the Three Wise Men as a gift for the Infant Jesus. Still a perennial Christmas favorite, the opera was shown annually on television for thirteen years.

Menotti's next opera, *The Saint of Bleeker Street,* lasted on Broadway for only ninety-two performances but it was critically acclaimed and won its composer his second Pulitzer Prize. It explored the spiritual dilemmas of simple Italians living in that ethnic neighborhood and caught up in a religious mystery they could not understand. Brooks Atkinson, an esteemed drama critic of the day, found that the "opera was sung, performed and staged with the mastery of the musical theater; it was the most powerful drama of the season."

Commercially successful or not, all of Menotti's twenty-odd operas are rich with genuine dramatic substance, heightened melodic expression and an intimacy of style and ambience more reminiscent of the theater than the operatic stage. Another notable innovation: the librettos and the orchestrations of his operas are distinctively and unmistakably his own.

His non-operatic works, such as symphonies, cantatas, concertos, ballet music, and librettos for a few Samuel Barber operas, all bear the stamp of his profound musicality, originality and forceful dramatic impact. *The Encyclopedia of the Opera* describes his style as "eclectic; it can be popular or esoteric, realistic or romantic—in any case, it meets the demands of good theater with remarkable effectiveness."

Menotti's prolific talents have often engaged him in seemingly overlapping or mutually exclusive pursuits. Early in 1958, for example, Samuel Barber's opera, *Vanessa,* premiered at the Metropolitan Opera House and Menotti contributed the libretto and the stage direction. Only a few years later, Menotti collaborated with Thomas Schippers in launching the "Festival of Two Worlds" in Spoleto, Italy, for the purpose of annually bringing together artists, known and unknown, native and foreign, and especially the young, for the presentation of original music, dance, poetry, drama. By 1991, the Festival had mushroomed incredibly; it drew 160,000 visitors at that time, had a nineteen-day-run and took in approximately $100,000 in liras. Its American offshoot in Charleston, South Carolina, known as "Spoleto, U.S.A.", has grown dramatically through the years. It benefits from the accumulated experience of the Spoleto Festivals in Europe.

The very concept, growth and success of the Spoleto

ventures is yet another tribute to Menotti's dedication to the artists of the world, as well as to the arts. Thus, just as the Pulitzer Prizes, the Guggenheim Fellowships, or a Cannes International Film Festival Award specifically acknowledge his artistic achievements, others celebrate as well his fostering of burgeoning or promising artists. In 1984, alone, he received two such awards: the Life Achievement Award from the National Italian American Foundation, and the Kennedy Center Performing Arts Award, generally regarded as the most important award in the field of the performing arts. Menotti's contribution is so extensive and varied—both quantitatively and qualitatively—that it challenges one's imagination.

In July of 1991, Menotti was summoned from his home in Scotland to Spoleto, Italy, to be feted on his eightieth birthday. Food and music galore, as one might expect, but there was also a hot-air balloon which descended periodically to deliver additional presents from friends and admirers. For Italians, in general, and for the people of Spoleto, in particular, Gian Carlo Menotti is the most popular opera composer since Puccini.

References: *Contemporary Authors,* Vol. 104, 1982.
Current Biography, H.W. Wilson & Co., 1979.
The Economist, July 20, 1991.
Connoisseur, January 1992.
Opera News, March 16, 1991.

Liza Minnelli

Liza Minnelli is indeed "a child of show-business my-thology," as she has often been called. Her greater-than-life parents were the extraordinarily talented actress and singer, Judy Garland, and the highly creative stage and motion-picture director, Vincente Minnelli.

When she was only two and a half, Liza made a walk-on appearance in one of her mother's movies, *In the Good Old Summertime;* five years later, she danced on the stage of the famous Palace Theater in New York as her mother sang "Swanee."

Most of her early years were spent in Hollywood where she often visited her parents' film sets in the MGM studio. As she grew up, she became more and more fascinated by virtually every aspect of film-making. "I'd learn all their (Astaire, Charisse, etc.) numbers," she has said, "then I'd go home and practice for hours in front of the mirror."

At sixteen, Liza first became seriously interested in an acting career, inspired by a musical, *Bye Bye Birdie,* which she saw on Broadway. She immediately joined the drama club in the school she was attending in Scarsdale, New York, and shortly after won the leading role in the drama club's staging of *The Diary of Anne Frank.* Though amateur, the production was impressive enough to attract a sponsor who paid for the students to tour Europe with the play.

Thus her roller-coaster career was launched, and Liza decided to drop out of school to concentrate on acting. She started modestly on Off-Broadway, as the third lead in a 1963 revival of *Best Foot Forward.* Then, after wildly successful appearances with her mother at the London Palladium, she became the youngest actress to win a Tony Award for her role in *Flora, the Red Menace.*

After the play's short run, Liza immediately set to work rehearsing a night-club act which opened in Washington, D.C., toured successfully in other cities, and broke all existing attendance records at the famous Persian Room in the Plaza Hotel in New York City. Her performance was enthusiastically received wherever she toured in the United States and abroad. The French dubbed her "La petite Piaf americaine."

Turning her energies temporarily to the cinema, Liza again proved her versatility by winning an Oscar nomination (1969) for her performance in *The Sterile Cuckoo* and, later, the Academy Award for Best Actress for her electrifying performance in *Cabaret*. It was when she was well into her third film, *Tell Me That You Love me, Junie Moon,* that her mother, Judy Garland, died. Again Liza assumed the role of head of the family in that crisis, making the funeral arrangements, looking after her siblings and settling her mother's estate.

After two grueling years on the road—in nightclubs, concert halls, theaters throughout the United States, and a world tour with her Tony Award-winning one-woman show—Liza appeared in two very different films: *That's Entertainment,* as one of the narrators, and in the animated feature, *Journey Back to Oz,* for which she provided the voice of Dorothy, the character Judy Garland had immortalized.

Liza hit her stride again as the female lead in Martin Scorsese's *New York, New York* (1977) which, she believes, represents the best acting she has ever done. However, since the box-office returns for that film, as well as the subsequent *Lucky Lady* and *A Matter of Time,* were less than rewarding, Liza returned briefly to the stage in *The Act,* for which she won her third Tony.

After appearing as narrator for the Martha Graham ballets at the Metropolitan Opera House in New York and the Royal House in London, Liza returned to the screen in 1981, in the very successful *Arthur* and then in its somewhat less popular sequel, *Arthur on the Rocks,* released many years later. On stage again in *The Rink,* she won another Tony nomination, but her role as the rebellious daughter was physically and emotionally exhausting and, as she explains, "like going through unguided analysis and diving into dangerous waters without any help!"

Perhaps that accounts largely for her emotional and psychological crisis during the run of the play, her increased dependence on valium and, ultimately, for her missing performances for the first time in her career. "I had no motivation, and I felt hopeless and helpless, and like I was dying," she told Stephen Williams of *Newsday,* some years later (July 24, 1985), after her recovery following detoxification and rehabilitation at the Betty Ford Center in California.

With her artist-husband, Mark Gero, she took a long vacation. She got back into gear with a six-month, twenty-seven-city "comeback" concert tour, beginning in June of 1985. Since then she has alternated television movies (notably, her Golden-Globe-winning-role in *Time to Live)*, with national and international concert tours, playing the London Palladium, New York City's Carnegie Hall, and Radio City Music Hall, and with countless television specials. In film, on stage, and in television, she has won critical acclaim, a multitude of fans, and recognition from her peers in show business, giving new dimension and credibility to the word "Superstar."

At the same time, Liza Minnelli has never lost sight of her ethnic heritage, participating in many Italian-American events, including fund-raisers for the flood-ravaged areas of Italy during the early 1970's.

Internationally, Liza has been awarded the British equivalent of the Oscar for Best Actress in 1972, along with Italy's coveted David di Donatello Award (for *The Sterile Cuckoo* and again for *Cabaret)*, and the Valentino Award.

In 1972, "Liza with a Z," received television's most prestigious award, the Emmy, for Most Outstanding Single Program—Variety and Popular Music. That same year she was named Female Star of the Year by the National Association of Theater Owners. Liza is the only woman to have received Las Vegas Entertainer of the Year honors for three consecutive years.

It must be said for this multitalented, hyperenergetic, charismatic child of legendary parents that, unlike many others with similar heritage, she has not rested nor coasted on their considerable laurels, but has chosen to work long and hard—one might even say, obsessively—to earn and merit her own.

References: Cawkwell and Smith, *The World Encyclopedia of the Film*, 1972.
Current Biography, 1988.
Ephraim Katz, *The Film Encyclopedia*, 1982.
Who's Who in America, 1988-1989.

John O. Pastore

Recognized and admired throughout the United States as one of the outstanding statesmen of the era, John Orlando Pastore is a credit to his heritage and to his home state of Rhode Island, where he was born March 17, 1907,

in Providence. He was the second of the five children of
Italian-born Michele and Erminia Asprinio Pastore. His
father, a tailor, died when John was nine, and for three
years his mother and older brother worked hard to provide
for the family. John did his share by assuming the house
chores and caring for his younger siblings.

Several years later, after his mother's re-marriage, John
continued to help by working after school as an errand
boy, as office boy in a law office, and foot-press operator
in a jewelry factory. His employers found him hard-working, conscientious and likable, as did his teachers in the
classical high school from which he was graduated with
honors in 1925.

The young graduate initially went to work as a claims
adjuster for the Narragansett Electric Company. Just two
years later, with his mother's encouragement, he enrolled
in an evening law course offered by Northeastern University, at a Providence branch. Pastore received his LL.B.
degree in 1931, and was admitted to the bar the following
year. He set up his first law office in the basement of the
family home.

After briefly practicing law, he decided to use his already proven oratorical skills and launched on a career in
politics. Accordingly, he not only got the Democratic
nomination for the State House of Representatives, but
also won the election in a district considered "strictly Republican." He was re-elected in 1936 and became chairman of the House Corporations Committee.

Between 1937 and 1939, with the Republicans in power, Pastore served on several committees, but with the return to a Democratic State administration in 1940, he was appointed assistant attorney-general in charge of the criminal calendar. In four years he was elected lieutenant-governor of Rhode Island and a year later (1945), he became governor and served two terms.

As governor, he showed integrity and fair-mindedness when he refused to build up his own political organization by appointing only Italian-Americans to office. He explained that he aspired to "build a record, not an organization." Among other equitable and progressive measures he sponsored were: a State anti-pollution authority, a direct primary, a fair employment-practice law, and others which won for him not only full Democratic support for re-election in 1948, but substantial Republican votes as well. After election, he canceled the traditional inaugural ball, explaining that since he had already been given one for his first term, a second one would be redundant and financially unfeasible.

Shortly thereafter, Pastore was chosen chairman of the six-man New England Governors' Conference, and again distinguished himself by proposing or supporting measures aimed at improving the public welfare and boosting the economy. A masterful orator and keen debater, he called for a uniform nationwide unemployment insurance tax and, with financial groups, tried to rectify conditions which were driving industry out of the State. He warned that he would veto any new taxes and he proposed pay increases for all State employees, excluding the Governor.

Later, in 1950, Pastore won a seat in the U.S. Senate, thus becoming, at forty-three, one of the youngest Senators and the first Italian-American ever elected to that body. A liberal on most domestic issues, Pastore supported the Kennedy and Johnson Administrations programs designed to eradicate poverty and discrimination in America. The *Washington Post* described him as "one of the best and most effective Congressional friends of Federal employees." He also held hearings on, and introduced, bills relating to cost-of-living increases and annual leave.

On international matters, Pastore denounced the treaty limitations on Italy's armed forces, which would weaken her as a member of the Italian Pact countries. During the 1952 campaign, he directed the Democratic Presidential and Congressional campaigns among Americans of Italian ancestry.

Originally, Senator Pastore backed President Johnson's defense spending and his conduct of the Vietnam War, and continued to support those policies during the early years of the Nixon Administration. In 1970, however, he not only voted for amendments aimed at ending the war, but also departed from his previous support of defense spending by joining an unsuccessful attempt to place a lowered ceiling on the Defense Department's appropriations for fiscal year 1971. Later, he endorsed the reduction of U.S. troop levels abroad and opposed the resumption of military aid to Turkey.

Throughout the Nixon-Ford years, Senator Pastore seldom strayed from his liberal position on domestic issues such as gun control, consumer protection, tax reforms, school desegregation. He also served and repeatedly chaired several committees, particularly the Joint Committee on Atomic Energy. After serving in the Senate for twenty-six years, Pastore retired in 1965, before the end of his term, to give his successor, Republican John Chaffee, seniority.

Not surprisingly, he received innumerable honorary degrees and awards during his years in office, and even after. Five of his honorary degrees are from Rhode Island colleges. He also has served as chairman of an American committee working with a group of Italian experts for the establishment of "Boys' Towns" in southern Italy.

Although still active in these and other ancillary professional and charitable pursuits, Senator Pastore in retirement can more fully enjoy his expanding family—his wife of fifty-one years, Elena Elizabeth Caito Pastore, and his children, Frances, Elizabeth, and Dr. John and their families.

When the NIAF honored the former Senator with an award in recognition of his achievements as a "statesman and role model," it also paid homage to his son, Dr. John Pastore, Jr., for his humanitarian activities in the "quest for peace." The venerable statesman thanked his wife, his former constituents, and the Foundation members, and brimming with paternal pride, he added, "my cup runneth over."

References: *Current Biography,* H & W Wilson Co., 1953.
Michael A. Musmanno, *The Story of the Italians in America,* Doubleday & Co., 1965.
E. W. Schoenenbaum, *Political Profiles—The Nixon-Ford Years,* 1979.
Who's Who in Government, 1972-73.

Jeno F. Paulucci

"If a concept is right, we can make it work," says Jeno F. Paulucci, a nationally recognized leader and innovator in the foods industry. His rags-to-riches success story is legend in the business world.

Jeno Paulucci was born in Aurora, Minnesota, on July 7, 1918. He is the son of Ettore and Michelina Buratti Paulucci, who migrated to Minnesota's Iron Range in 1912, from Belisio Solfare, Province of Pesaro, Italy. Jeno spent his childhood in Hibbing, where his father was an iron-ore miner and his family operated a neighborhood grocery. He attended Hibbing Junior College as a pre-law student until he realized there was more opportunity for him in marketing and sales.

Jeno's style is unique. He started the Chun King Corporation on a $2500 loan and brought the company to world leadership in its field. Twenty years later, in 1966, he sold it to R.J. Reynolds Tobacco Company for 63-million dollars in cash. He became the first Chairman of the Board and co-founder of R.J. Reynolds Foods, now RJR-Nabisco. Immediately after the sale, he founded Jeno's Inc., which blossomed into national leadership among Italian foods with famous "Jeno's Pizza Rolls." The company now belongs to Pillsbury.

Although nearing his seventy-fifth birthday, Paulucci recently established two new national companies: Luigino's, Inc., to produce frozen Italian entrees under the Michelina's brand (named for his mother who gave him the recipes), and Pasta Lovers Trattorias, a franchise chain of casual Italian restaurants.

Jeno Paulucci is Chairman of the Board of Paulucci International, a family investment group which directs independent business and commercial properties' interests and investments nationally and internationally. He is also Chairman of Paulucci Estates, Sanford, Florida, which broke ground in November, 1982, for the 500-million-dollar Heathrow, a beautiful, exclusive planned community near Disney World in Central Florida.

Paulucci attributes his magic touch to "hard work by dedicated people." While he has achieved phenomenal growth with unique and revolutionary products, and with their packaging and merchandising, he has developed other interests. He formed and is Chairman of Jeno F. Paulucci & Associates of Florida, Inc., an advertising, public relations and research agency. He is also Chairman of Central Produce and Equipment, Sanford, Florida.

Until its sale in 1982, Paulucci was Chairman of The Cornelius Company, Minneapolis, Minnesota, the leading worldwide manufacturer of food and beverage dispensing equipment. Over the course of his business career, he held the major interest in First Sierra Mutual Fund.

In 1969, Grosset & Dunlap (New York), published Paulucci's business autobiography, *How It Was To Make $100,000,000 in a Hurry.* The book was reprinted in Italian by Rizzoli Publications for distribution in Europe.

The Paulucci Family Foundation, which he has endowed for worthwhile civic and charitable work, is noted for its many acts of philanthropy. Always a crusader and concerned about the economic well-being of his fellow residents of north-eastern Minnesota, Jeno founded NEMO, Inc., (North East Minnesota Organization for Economic

Education) through which he spearheaded a state-wide campaign for passage of the Taconite Constitutional Amendment that induced private investment of $2-billion in Minnesota's ailing mining region. This created 20,000 jobs and more than $2-billion more in tax revenues, dedicated to the region's future under terms of Minnesota's "Paulucci Bill."

Through a grant in excess of $200,000 from Jeno, NEMO co-ordinated a comprehensive study of Minnesota taxation and natural resources to develop a "Blueprint for Minnesota"—a multimillion-dollar economic development program. It also fostered the planning and construction of the $6,700,000 Duluth Arena-Auditorium. The Jeno and Lois Paulucci Family Foundation provided a feasibility study for the establishment of a $4,400,000 Recreation-Convention Center addition to the complex. In like manner, Jeno personally financed the community's share of the feasibility funds project for a new air-terminal complex and industrial park associated with Duluth International Airport, completed in 1974. He was instrumental in obtaining numerous federal and state grants for other improvements and has been the catalyst and investor not only in Duluth, but also in Sanford, Florida.

Jeno Paulucci is a man who cares and is dedicated to the responsibilities of life in our changing America. He is a champion of the American system. Although politically active, he is always independent and has never held, sought, nor does he want public office. He has declined appointment by two presidents to Cabinet offices and an ambassadorship. He feels he can serve his fellow man better by remaining outside political structures. Nevertheless, he has counseled White House Administrations on economic problems in the United States; served as liaison between the White House and Rome to arrange economic conferences and was presidential emissary to evaluate United States disaster-relief efforts in Italy in 1976 and 1980. Proud of his Italian heritage, he is founder and has been Chairman of the National Italian American Foundation, Washington, D.C., since its organization in 1975. He is considered a primary spokesman for the nation's twenty-five-million Italian-Americans. In 1990 he received the Ellis Island Congressional Medal of Honor for his outstanding contributions to those who share his heritage.

His state and national honors for humanitarianism, citizenship and contributions to civic development are legion. Just a few of the outstanding honors Jeno Paulucci received as an Italian-American are: UNICO National Rizzuto Gold Medal, Order of Merit from the Republic of Italy, guest of President Johnson on Liberty Island at the signing of the Immigration Reform law. Duluth, Minnesota, elevated him to its Hall of Fame. He received many honors: several Doctor of Law honorary degrees; Man of the Year, Executive of the Year, Businessman of the Year. In 1972, he was selected United States Employer of the Year among all major corporations.

Jeno Paulucci is a champion of free enterprise who also demands that business meet its responsibilities; a benefactor who insists on and creates opportunity for the disadvantaged; a decisive leader who makes things happen. His words will long be remembered: "To hell with committee meetings. Think, Act, Expedite and Push It Thru Yourself! ... I cannot give you the formula for success, but I can give you the formula for failure: Try to Please Everybody! ... It isn't easy to change a sick society ... But if we speak out, if we become involved, believe me ... we will find no greater joy or satisfaction than knowing that we are working to make a contribution to our fellow man."

Truly a man of ideas, Jeno F. Paulucci is dedicated to results. He makes things happen. His dream is embodied in Heathrow where he has combined all the elements of a com-munity—business, commercial, and residential—in a single, planned city with social and cultural enrichment and quality of life which can result from planned evolution.

References: *Jeno F. Paulucci,* Three-page narrative biography, 1992.
The Perfect Community, Update on Heathrow, Florida,
1992.
Who's Who in America, 1986-1987.

Edmund D. Pellegrino

Currently President of the prestigious Catholic University of America, Washington, D.C., Dr. Pellegrino is a highly respected physician, educator and author, as well. He was born in Newark, New Jersey, June 22, 1920, son of Michael J. and Marie Catone Pellegrino.

After his graduation from Xavier High School, New York, young Pellegrino matriculated at St. John's University, New York, and was graduated *summa cum laude*, with a B.S. degree in 1941. Three years later he received his M.D. degree from New York University.

After serving residencies in medicine at Bellevue, Goldwater Memorial and Homer Folks Tuberculosis Hospitals, he was a research Fellow in Renal Medicine and Physiology at New York University. He successively held numerous highly responsible positions as Founding Chairman and Director, or Founding Dean and Professor, Chancellor, President, of outstanding Medical Centers in New Jersey, Kentucky, Memphis and New Haven. Recently, he has been serving as Director of the Georgetown University Center for the Advanced Study of Ethics and Director of the Center for Clinical Bioethics at the same university. Dr. Pellegrino also teaches there as Professor of Medicine and Medical Ethics.

Off campus and on, he is Fellow or Member of twenty scientific, professional and honorary societies, including the Institute of Medicine of the National Academy of Sciences, the Association of American Physicians, and the American Clinical and Climatological Association. He has been the recipient of thirty-eight honorary doctoral degrees and countless awards, including the National Italian American Lifetime Achievement Award in 1980.

Dr. Pellegrino's publications are similarly impressive for their content and scope. He has written over 400 items: editorial contributions, articles and reviews in medical science, philosophy and ethics. He is also the founding editor of the *Journal of Medicine and Philosophy.*

His *Humanism and the Physician* was published in 1979 by the University of Tennessee Press. More recently, Dr. Pellegrino, together with David Thomasma, Ph.D., wrote *Philosophical Basis of Medical Practice* (1981), and *For the Patient's Good* (1988). Both books were published by Oxford University Press.

Married in 1944, Dr. Pellegrino and his wife, the former Clementine Coakley, have six children: Thomas, Stephen, Virginia, Michael, Andrea, and Leah.

References: *The Journal of the American Medical Association* March 13, 1991, June 19, 1991. *Who's Who in America,* 1992-1993.

Peter W. Rodino, Jr.

Although Congressman Rodino served in Congress from the 81st to the 91st, he is remembered principally as chairman of the House Judiciary hearings during the 1974 Watergate proceedings.

Peter Rodino was born in Newark, New Jersey, on June 7, 1909. His parents were Peter and Margaret Gerard Rodino—his father, a bricklayer who had emigrated from southern Italy. Young Peter grew up in a tough neighborhood where gunfire in the streets was a familiar occurrence.

At a time when first-generation Italian Americans found discouraging stumbling blocks, especially in the pursuit of higher education, Peter Rodino persevered and was accepted at the University of Newark. He went on to the New Jersey School of Law (now Rutgers University) where he was awarded his LL.B. degree in 1938. Although he set up his law practice in Newark soon after, Rodino volunteered for military service even before the United States entered World War II. A few weeks after Pearl Harbor, he and Marianna Stango were married. That union was to be blessed with two children, Margaret and Peter.

Rodino served in combat with the First Armored Division in North Africa and Italy until his discharge in 1946. In recognition of his superior achievements, he was awarded many honors, including the Bronze Star, the War Cross, the Knights of the Order of the Crown (Italy).

Within two years of his discharge, Rodino was elected to Congress where he represented most of Newark and several surrounding communities. Thus began his distinguished career of more than forty years as congressman.

A strong supporter of immigration reform, Rodino was influential in the passage in the House of a Johnson Administration bill that eliminated the existing nationality quota system of immigration control and provided for the enactment of equitable and unbiased immigration laws for members of all ethnic groups. Rodino considered the Immigration Reform and Control Act of 1966 the end of a discriminatory system that had dimmed "the welcoming beacon of America as a place of hope and opportunity for people throughout the world."

Peter Rodino strongly backed civil rights legislation, acting as floor manager for the open-housing provision of the Civil Rights Act of 1966.

He also compiled an outstanding voting record in consumer protection legislation, such as, the 1969 bill (The Philadelphia Plan), which called for the government to force the hiring of minority workers for federally-financed projects.

In 1975, Rodino voted for the legalization of common-site picketing for workers striking a single subcontractor and also for a federal loan guarantee for financially strapped New York City. About that time, too, he authored the legislation that made Columbus Day a nationwide holiday.

Rodino's record in the early years of the 1970s was that of a very well-thought-of-representative, who had taken the lead in a number of key domestic issues. However, Rodino's place in American history was about to take a giant step forward.

For Peter Rodino was thrust into one of the most challenging legislative roles in our national history—the chairmanship of the impeachment hearings for President Richard Nixon. As chairman of the Judiciary Committee, Rodino had a contentious crew of legislators—some anxious to defend Nixon at any cost, others equally determined to remove the president. Rodino's job was to meld these highly intelligent and determined legislators into a fair and honest panel that would decide the truth of the charges against President Nixon. Failure to do so could have brought calamity and acrimony for decades to the country. But Peter Rodino did not fail.

The time was right for partisan politics but Rodino set a tone of dignity and decorum and his committeemen followed his lead despite the potentially explosive situation which might well have degenerated into a witch hunt.

Accordingly, when sufficient evidence had been gathered to justify impeachment and President Nixon obviated the procedure by a timely resignation, Rodino did not agree with the many House members who called for impeachment hearings to be resumed after Gerald Ford's Presidential pardon of Nixon.

Rodino strongly objected, contending that impeachment was intended to remove Nixon from office, and should not be used to accomplish any other purpose, such as harassing an ex-President. This courageous action further removed partisanship from this most difficult period in American history.

In his book, *U.S. v. Richard Nixon*, Frank Mankiewicz observed that Rodino and his committee "had done the job the constitution had assigned them, and they had achieved—in the great conflict dividing Americans between the president and the Constitution, between the arrogance of power and the rule of law—a measure of peace and honor."

Following the impeachment hearings, Congressman Rodino continued his dedicated service and retired only after that service had reached 40 years. When asked what progress he thought his fellow Italian-Americans had made during that interim, he replied, "I think we can all be proud that Italo-Americans have achieved prominence in every field from public service to science and education. And let's not forget an Italian American was the Democratic Party's vice presidential candidate in 1984." He added that his own story in many ways was "the story of the great promise and opportunity of America."

His colleagues, constituents and non-partisan admirers would add that Peter Rodino, himself, is an inspiring example of the political behavior of the sons of immigrants —of whatever origins they might be.

An award-winning journalist Michael Barone has written in *The Almanac of American Politics*, "The strength of the American political system is that it has produced people of extraordinary talent who have happened to find their way into crucial positions at critical times and who have performed far better than their records would have sug-

gested. Such leaders sometimes come from the most un-
likely places: a Lincoln from the western hick town of
Springfield, Illinois; a Franklin Roosevelt from the aristo-
cratic patron families of the Hudson Valley. Within that
tradition is Peter Rodino, from Newark, New Jersey."

References: Drew, Elizabeth: *Washington Journal,* 1973-74.
        Washington Newsletter, "Interview," July 1988.
        Who's Who in America, 1975.

Peter Sammartino

Dr. Peter Sammartino—founder, president, and chancellor emeritus of Fairleigh Dickinson University —epitomizes a success story that has few equals in the history of higher education. His career as an educator is one of the most distinguished in America.

His experiences during the 1930's as a participant in the experimental New College movement at Teachers College, Columbia University, served him well. He applied these ideas to the multiple-campus expansion of the University he founded in 1941. No other educator has been so intimately involved with the philosophy, experimentation, and administration of higher education for half a century.

At the beginning of the twentieth century, Gaetano and Eva Amendola Sammartino emigrated from Salerno, Italy, to the United States. Their first child, Peter, was born in New York on August 15, 1904. He graduated from the College of the City of New York in 1924, received his Ph.D. from New York University in 1931, and then studied at the Sorbonne in Paris. He married Sylvia, the daughter of Anna Bianchi and Louis Joseph Scaramelli, a prominent and successful businessman in Rutherford, New Jersey. Among Peter Sammartino's many books dedicated to Sally, the most significant dedication is found in *Of Castles and Colleges* (1972): "To my wife, Sally, who has always done half of the work but who has rarely gotten any of the credit."

Sally Scaramelli Sammartino collaborated with Peter in all his endeavors at Fairleigh Dickinson University for fifty years. It became America's eighth largest privately supported university. Together they were instrumental in the development of five college campuses in New Jersey, one in England (Wroxton in the Cotswolds), and one at

St. Croix, Virgin Islands—a marine biological laboratory. They also had the vision to start New Jersey's first dental school at Fairleigh Dickinson University. They visited and assisted colleges and universities in twenty-one countries throughout Africa, Asia and Europe.

Peter Sammartino received honorary degrees from colleges and universities in five countries and has been honored by seven others. President Lyndon Johnson appointed him to the Advisory Board of the Peace Corps, and President Richard Nixon appointed him to the Board of Foreign Scholarships. In 1966 he became Vice President of the New Jersey Constitutional Convention and was chairman of the International Committee of the New Jersey Bicentennial Commission. Twice he was awarded the silver medal of the Sons of the American Revolution for restoring old historic houses in New Jersey.

As an international educator, Dr. Peter Sammartino disseminated culture, promoted research and scholarship, and spearheaded several literary and historical institutions in the metropolitan area, such as: American Institute of Italian Studies, American Society of the Italian Legions of Merit, House of Savoy Archival Center Committee. Not only was Dr. Sammartino founder-president of the International Association of University Presidents, but he was also the national chairman of the International Christopher Columbus Quincentennial Commission. Among his thirty books, the founder of Fairleigh Dickinson University also wrote *Columbus*—a study of his life and accomplishments—in order to promote interest in the 1992 Columbus Celebrations.

In 1974, instead of being concerned with his retirement, Peter and Sally Sammartino began a nationwide campaign and ultimately convinced Congress to authorize funds for the restoration of Ellis Island. The idea came to Peter while touring the abandoned tract of United States government property which was once the "Gateway to America." His parents had landed on Ellis Island after a long voyage from Italy. Remembering that it had been a "clearing house" for more than sixteen-million immigrants, tears came to his eyes in a sudden burst of emotion. He planted the "seed" for the restoration and obtained the first grant of $1,500,000, which was followed by an additional $5,000,000, toward restoring America's most famous shrine.

Peter Sammartino coped with the many human problems involved with building, equipping, staffing and integrating Fairleigh Dickinson University. He was interested in the issues of student freedom, sex on campus, optimal nutrition in college cafeterias, athletics, and fund-raising. He promoted foreign travel for students and entertained foreign and native dignitaries. He lent his expertise in dealing with situations regarding labor unions and involving parents of students. He and Sally cared enough about the students to know each one personally. When they retired in 1967, Fairleigh Dickinson University boasted 20,000 students, fifty-two buildings, and seven campuses valued at $250,000,000 with an endowment of $62,000,000 consisting of stocks, bonds, and real estate.

When asked to name four things that make life worth-while, Peter Sammartino said: "Serving others, communicating with people, feeling exhilaration at beauty, and being able to create." He was always innovative not only in his approach to teaching, but also in thinking of ways to solve problems.

While visiting the Teaneck Campus cafeteria one day, he noticed that students were having difficulty trying to manage their lunch trays and briefcases while going through the cafeteria lines. Several days later while in New York City having his portrait painted, the artist's hand-carved palette kept attracting his attention. Suddenly he got an idea. Why not have a hole in the triangular tray at the campus cafeteria, so that a student could rest it on his arm, poke his fingers through the hole in order to balance it, and still manage to carry a briefcase in his right hand? Two weeks later trays with holes in them appeared in the cafeteria. He registered the name "Tray Angles" and applied for a patent, arranging with the manufacturer that all future profits from the sale of this item be placed in a scholarship fund for the college. The Sammartinos were interested in their students and loved them. They believed that, when students are challenged by a competent teacher, they enjoy the learning experience and profit all the more from it.

A staunch promoter of the Italian contribution to the creation of the United States of America, Dr. Sammartino always advocated studies in Italian culture. In fact, as a student in 1929, he organized the Verdi Choral Society in New York City which exists today as the Coro d'Italia. He was one of the group of students responsible for the establishment of the Casa Italiana of Columbia University and he organized the first Italian Honors Society.

In his later years, Dr. Sammartino donated his voluminous library of rare books on Italian-Americans and Italian culture to the Casa Italiana Zerilli-Marimò of the New York University—his Alma Mater. This collection is one of the best in the United States.

Not only did he spearhead the Philip Mazzei Project at Fairleigh Dickinson University, but he also encouraged studies on Giuseppe Garibaldi, William Paca, and other Italian patriots and explorers. As Vice President of the Northeastern Region of the National Italian American Foundation, which he had helped establish, Dr. Sammartino sponsored seminars and conferences in an effort to disseminate Italian culture in the United States.

Sammartino's book, *I Dreamed a College,* was the basis for the film featuring Peter and Sally Sammartino on the Fairleigh Dickinson University campuses. Working together harmoniously they set the tone for the academic, social and cultural lifestyle of the first twenty-five years of Fairleigh Dickinson University. Their zest for history, literature, philosophy, and their interest in music, art, and science have been an inspiration to all. They are indeed legendary for their charity, dedication and commitment to society.

On March 29, 1992, Peter and Sally Sammartino died. Governor James Florio expressed the condolence of the entire State of New Jersey: "The Sammartinos lived their lives with purpose, committed to the values which define our species as compassionate, civilized and humane. Their devotion to education, the arts, and the humanities will have lasting effects on our State and beyond."

Peter Sammartino was always an internationalist and yearned for a world organization which could enhance communication among educators world-wide. An innovator and visionary, his dream became a reality in 1964: with typical decisiveness and flair, he founded the International Association of University Presidents. Today, the group consists of over 600 university presidents from over fifty countries, organized into regional councils and allied with the United Nations. The IAUP Executive Committee, meeting in Bangkok in July, 1992, "saluted Dr. Sammartino for his pioneering achievement, and expressed its gratitude for the founding of an organization which has become a world force."

As a sign of their love for the youth of America, not only did the Sammartinos establish "The Peter and Sylvia Sammartino Charitable Remainder Unitrust," but they bequeathed their estate to Fairleigh Dickinson University in order to provide scholarships for students interested in the teaching profession. Thus countless young men and women will continue to benefit from the wisdom, dedication, and generosity of the founders of Fairleigh Dickinson University.

References: Emil Lengyel-Heinz F. Mackensen, *The First Quarter Century, A History of Fairleigh Dickinson University,* 1942-1967, A.S. Barnes & Co., 1974.
Peter Sammartino, *I Dreamed a College,* A.S. Barnes & Co., 1977.
Peter Sammartino, *Of Castles and Colleges, Notes toward an Autobiography,* A.S. Barnes & Co., 1972.
Helen L. Warren-Richard W. Holub, *Fairleigh Dickinson University: A Pictorial History, 1942-1967,* The Crispen Co., 1980.
Margherita Marchione, *Peter and Sally Sammartino (Biographical Notes),* Cornwall Books, 1994.

Antonin Scalia

Antonin Scalia, the first Italian-American to serve as Justice of the United States Supreme Court, was born in Trenton, New Jersey, March 11, 1936 and was raised in Queens, New York. His mother, Catherine Louise Panaro, was a first-generation Italian-American. His father, S. Eugene Scalia, had emigrated from Sicily when he was fifteen years old. Both his parents became educators: his mother taught elementary school and his father became professor of Romance Languages at Brooklyn College. From his earliest school years, they had reason to be proud of their only child, Nino.

By the time he had entered Xavier High School in New York City, a Jesuit military school, young Scalia had clearly evinced his unusual scholastic abilities, but not to the exclusion of extracurricular interests and activities. He was first in his class at graduation, a lieutenant-colonel in the school regiment, and director of the marching band.

Subsequently, he matriculated at Georgetown University and when he graduated in 1957, it was again as the Number One student. Richard Coleman, a classmate at Georgetown, has remained his close friend for more than thirty years. He observes that Scalia's schooling, which included six years of Latin and five of Greek, gave him an historical and philosophical perspective matched by few others.

At Harvard Law School, Scalia again proved himself scholastically, and became Note Editor of the *Law Review*. At Harvard, too, he met Radcliffe student Maureen McCarthy whom he married in 1960, the same year as his graduation. Nine children would be born to the Scalias.

His first job was with the prestigious law firm of Jones, Day, Cockley and Reavis in Cleveland, Ohio. Although he steadily rose in the ranks of the firm, Scalia passed up a profitable partnership, opted for the intellectual life, and accepted a position as law professor at the University of Virginia, where he taught from 1967-1971.

In 1971, Scalia went to Washington, D.C., first as general counsel of the White House Office of Telecommunications Policy, then as Chairman of the Administrative Conference of the United States, and finally as Assistant Attorney General in charge of the Justice Department's Office of Legal Counsel. He returned again to academia from 1977 to 1982 when he taught at the University of Chicago Law School and, as visiting professor, at the Stanford Law School and at the Georgetown Law Center.

During that same period Scalia, a valued specialist in administrative law, was named editor of *Regulation,* the magazine published by the American Enterprise Institute for Public Policy Research. As it happened, deregulation, which President Reagan pushed as a policy, was of considerable interest to Scalia, who largely shared the President's conservatism.

Accordingly, the Reagan administration tapped Scalia for a judgeship on the Federal Appeals Court in Washington, D.C., and he served in that capacity from 1982 to 1986. When the President nominated him as associate justice of the United States Supreme Court, he rode out the usual Capitol Hill probes, sailed smoothly through the Senate hearings and was confirmed 98-0. Thus the son of an Italian immigrant became the first law professor named to the Supreme Court since Wiley Rutledge in 1943.

However, upon accepting the Public Service Achievement Award presented to him in 1988 by the National Italian American Foundation, Justice Scalia gave a different slant to the story of his success: he saw it as a proof of what an extraordinary country the United States is in making it possible for "the son of a man who came over when he was 15 years old ... to rise to that high a post in government."

Although a relative newcomer to the nation's highest court, Justice Scalia has already distinguished himself not only as an eminent authority on constitutional law, but also as an aggressive interrogator, an articulate advocate and an intellectual dynamo.

Ethan Bonner, the respected writer for the *Boston Globe,* is not alone in considering him possibly "the most important justice of the new judicial era"; similarly, Robert Nagel of the University of Colorado School of Law feels that "Justice Scalia's impact on the law will be felt over the decades."

Notably, Scalia's crusades are vehemently against judicial overreaching, especially when the Supreme Court trespasses on legislative terrain. He adamantly believes legislatures, not courts, should rule on a terminally ill patient's right to die, on whether the public schools have the right to teach "creation science," or whether criminals who are clearly guilty should be allowed to go free on technicalities. He is convinced the Supreme Court should play a less dramatic role in the daily life of the average American and leave related matters to the discretion and regulation of the Legislative branch—as our tripartite division of powers originally intended.

In short, Justice Scalia is fighting to restore judges to their proper place in American life—interpreting laws, not making them. For if America allows itself to be increasingly governed by an "imperial judiciary," eventually most major decisions on how we live will be removed from the democratic process.

Although he terms himself "a thoughtful moderate," Justice Scalia's conservative positions are often diametrically at odds with the viewpoint of progressives and liberals—on the constitutional power of legislatures to adopt abortion restrictions, for example, or on the legality of race-based preferential hiring. Whether or not one agrees with such—and other equally controversial—positions, there can be no doubt about his sincerity of purpose, his integrity, and his abiding commitment to what he perceives to be the fundamental laws and principles of the United States.

Yet, despite such grave responsibilities in the most solemn of professional environments, Justice Scalia is far from the stodgy, reclusive, unapproachable stereotype one might expect. This might be explained, in part, by his Italian heritage but also by his fulfilling marriage and the incredibly humanizing and lightening-up effect of a brood of nine.

As a result, he comes across as gregarious, ebullient, charming and scintillating in his social life and, professionally, as a powerful, passionate and forthright public speaker, an intellectual giant and an unconventional judge, neither sedate nor reserved, but often tempering his judgments with wit and candor. Already the most provocative Justice in the Supreme Court, he admits that being a conscientious judge is far from easy. "The hardest part," he admits, "is not mistaking your own views for the law. I am not comfortable with imposing my moral views on the society. ... Perhaps no conscientious judge ever succeeds entirely."

Given his proven record for integrity, objectivity and humane-ness, Justice Scalia comes comfortably close to the ideal.

References: *Newsweek,* "Sparring on the Bench," December 11, 1989; "The Court's Mr. Right," May 11, 1990.
Readers' Digest, "Top Gun on the High Court" by Fred Barnes, July 1991.
The Supreme Court Yearbook, "Antonin Scalia," 1989-1990.
U. S. News, "Reigning in Citizens' Rights," December 16,1991.

Frank Sinatra

Frank Sinatra is a perennially popular and dominant force in the entertainment industry. He has long been acclaimed as the world's leading performer of popular music—the artist who set the mold for all others to fill. And he is, of course, more than a singer—Frank Sinatra is also an actor, recording artist, cabaret and concert star, radio and television personality and, on occasion, a producer, director and conductor. His career, which includes acting roles in more than fifty films, some of which he produced and directed, is studded with accolades: Oscars, Grammys, Emmys and the prestigious Peabody Award. A dedicated humanitarian, Mr. Sinatra has received numerous honors and awards in appreciation of his charitable endeavors.

A performer for more than five decades, Sinatra began a year-long Diamond Jubilee World Tour on December 11, 1990, the eve of his seventy-fifth birthday. Both concerts were performed at Meadowlands' Brendan Byrne Arena, just five miles from Hoboken, New Jersey, where Frank Sinatra was born and began his spectacular career. His life in recent years has been marked by prodigious activity in concerts, recordings, cabaret appearances and film.

Frank Sinatra made his first record on July 13, 1939, with Harry James and his Orchestra, for Brunswick Records at a New York City studio that is now part of CBS Records. With this record, "From the Bottom Of My Heart" and "Melancholy Mood," and his recording of "All or Nothing at All," as well as his later debut as a band singer, Sinatra changed the face of popular music in America and paved the way for others to follow. His 1988-89 Ultimate Event world tour, with Liza Minnelli and Sammy Davis, Jr., consistently broke box-office records at arenas and theaters in the United States, Japan, Australia and Europe. Their forty-five concerts played to audience and critical acclaim in twenty-nine cities throughout the world.

Among Sinatra's honors are the Presidential Medal of Freedom, the nation's highest award, received at a White House ceremony; an honorary Doctorate of Engineering from the Stevens Institute of Technology in Hoboken, New Jersey; and Austria's Medal of Honor for Science and Art, First Class, which he received following his benefit in Vienna to aid handicapped children.

Sinatra has performed at Rio de Janeiro's Maracana Soccer Stadium before the largest audience (175,000) ever to attend a concert by a soloist (the event is recorded in the Guinness Book of World Records). He served as producer and director of entertainment for President Reagan's Inaugural Galas in 1981 and 1985. He also appeared in several successful annual engagements at Carnegie Hall, each surpassing the previous year in critical acclaim and box office records at the fabled New York landmark.

During his illustrious career, Sinatra acquired such famous nicknames as "The Chairman of the Board," "The Voice," "The Greatest Roman of Them All " and, of course, " Ol' Blue Eyes." The world knows that he was born Francis Albert Sinatra, of Italian parents, December 12, 1915, in Hoboken, New Jersey. As a youngster, he had visions of a sportswriting career and worked briefly as a copy boy for a local newspaper. However, that ambition was short-lived once he heard the unique music styles of Billie Holiday and Bing Crosby. He decided to pursue a singing career and teamed with a local group called the Hoboken Four. It didn't last very long and, when the quartet broke up, the young singer took the solo route and toured the vaudeville circuit. In 1937, Sinatra worked as a singing MC at the Rustic Cabin, in Englewood, New Jersey. His talent attracted Harry James, who hired him as a band vocalist. It was 1939, the heyday of the big bands and Frank Sinatra was on his way. Within a year, he joined Tommy Dorsey and began recording with the band's vocal group, the Pied Pipers.

Sinatra later struck out on his own and appeared on radio's "Your Hit Parade" and his own show, "Songs By Sinatra." In late 1942, he made an historic appearance at the old Paramount Theater on Times Square. The head-liner on the bill was Benny Goodman and when the bandleader introduced Frank Sinatra, the audience erupted and cheered itself hoarse. There was dancing in the aisles, whistling, whooping and shrieking. It was the beginning of a long love affair between the singer and his fans. It was one of the most spectacular events in show-business history and Sinatra's career soared.

He made his movie debut the next year and went on to appear in more than fifty films, among them, *Anchors Aweigh, On The Town, Guys and Dolls, Pal Joey,* and *The Manchurian Candidate. From Here to Eternity* brought him an Academy Award as Best Supporting Actor, for his memorable portrayal of Angelo Maggio, the skinny, feisty soldier stationed in Hawaii. He was nominated for an Oscar for his role as a drug addict in *The Man With the Golden Arm.* In 1946 he received a special Oscar for *The House I Live in,* the documentary that made an eloquent plea for an end to prejudice of all kinds.

In 1953, Sinatra joined Capitol Records and began an association that lasted seven years and proved to be one of the most successful the recording industry has ever seen. Some of his most famous and well-liked recordings came during these years, marked by arrangements by Nelson Riddle and Gordon Jenkins. Among those songs that have become American classics are "I've Got the World on a String," "I Get a Kick Out of You," "In the Wee Small Hours of the Morning," "The Lady Is a Tramp," "Witchcraft" and "Young at Heart." Sinatra received numerous honors and distinctions during this period.

During the 1960's, Sinatra established his own recording company, Reprise Records, and released a number of well-remembered hit albums. He also starred in several award-winning one-man TV specials.

The decade of the '70s was highlighted by new albums, film roles, U.S. and international tours, a record-breaking Broadway engagement with Count Basie and Ella Fitzgerald, television movies and music specials, and, in 1979, the celebration of his 40th anniversary in show business, taped as a special for NBC-TV.

During the past few years he has continued to make appearances throughout this country and abroad (Japan, England, Australia, Finland, France, Austria, Norway, Germany, Egypt, South America, Italy, Spain), performed on a number of television specials, and released critically and popularly acclaimed albums. In 1986, MGM/UA Home Video brought out "Portrait of an Album," a video cassette documenting the making of his album, "L.A. is My Lady." His recording of "New York, New York," has become New York City's national anthem, is played at home games for both the Yankees and Mets, and is met with cheers and standing ovations throughout the world.

In 1978, he went to Israel for the dedication of the Frank Sinatra International Student Centre at the Mount Scopus campus of the Hebrew University; another building in Israel named for him is the Frank Sinatra Youth Centre in Nazareth. The following year Sinatra returned to the Middle East, performing a benefit concert in Egypt at the request of Madam Sadat for her favorite charity.

Frank Sinatra continues to receive honors of distinction. Variety Clubs International, a show-business charity, saluted him for his achievements as an entertainer and a humanitarian. The event, which was attended by scores of celebrity friends, was a CBS-TV special. As a tribute, the Sinatra Family Children's Unit for the Chronically Ill was established at the Seattle Children's Orthopedic Hospital and Medical Center. He was one of the five distinguished honorees (the others were Jimmy Stewart, Elia

Kazan, Virgil Thompson and Katherine Dunham) at the 1983 Kennedy Center Honors.

Still Abbot of the New York Friars Club, Sinatra has made a special appearance in Chicago at the city's annual Chicago Fest and headlined a concert at the opening of a new 5000-seat amphitheater in Altos de Chavon, in the Dominican Republic, that was taped by Paramount Video. The concert continues to be broadcast on television systems throughout the country. He has also been inducted into the National Broadcasters Hall of Fame. Peter Gammon, writing in *The Oxford Companion to Popular Music,* says of Sinatra: "He has probably been the most vital artist, the most popular singer, the most magnetic personality, and the greatest lyric interpreter in the pre-rock years of popular music."

In addition to concert tours throughout the world, his activities have included a six-hour television mini-series on his life, produced by his daughter, Tina, for Warner Brothers and aired on CBS-TV. Frank Sinatra's pasta sauce, Sugo da Tavola, debuted on supermarket shelves, was the first of a line of signature Italian food products inspired by family recipes.

Despite a hectic schedule of professional commitments, Frank Sinatra somehow manages to find the time to lend his talents to humanitarian causes, performing benefit concerts in the United States and overseas and participating in numerous fund-raising drives. Among the organizations which have benefited from his activities are the Red

Cross, Palm Springs' Desert Hospital, Variety Clubs International, the New York PAL, Cabrini Medical Center, the World Mercy Fund, and the National Multiple Sclerosis Society. He has always quietly provided personal financial aid to friends and private individuals in need.

A particular charity favorite is the Barbara Sinatra Children's Center at Eisenhower Medical Center in Palm Springs, California. His wife, Barbara, is the driving force behind the facility which treats victims of sexual, physical and emotional abuse. Both Sinatras have been actively involved in the Center's activities since its opening in 1986.

On January 9, 1993, Frank Sinatra received the prestigious Desert Palm Achievement Award at the Palm Springs International Film Festival. Many of his screen performances were spotlighted to celebrate his memorable career.

References: Nowland & Nowland, *Movie Characters of Leading Performers of the Sound Era,* American Library Association, 1990.

The New York Times, May 17, June 8, October 7, December 9, 1990.

The Oxford Companion to Popular Music. Oxford University Press, 1991.

John Joseph Sirica

John Joseph Sirica was named "Man of the Year" by *Time Magazine* (January 7, 1974). He was born in Water-bury, Connecticut, on March 19, 1904. His father, Federico Sirica, was seven years old when, in 1887, he emigrated from a small village near Naples. He married Rosa Zinno from New Haven, Connecticut. They worked hard to make ends meet: Federico was a barber and his wife ran a small grocery store. They had high ideals for their children, John and Andrew.

Life was not easy for the Sirica family as they moved from Ohio to Georgia, from New Orleans to Los Angeles, from Richmond, Virginia to Washington, D.C. "It was an uphill fight against poverty," John Sirica used to say in his talks to students. "If I made it, you too can make it." He succeeded in overcoming financial difficulties and earned his law degree in 1926, from Georgetown University.

He joined a Washington law firm, was a counsel for a congressional committee and became interested in Republican Party affairs. In 1957, President Eisenhower appointed Sirica to the Federal Bench.

Sirica was never afraid or ashamed of any type of work in order to provide for his family. To finance his education, he had worked part-time as a boxing coach for the Knights of Columbus, even though his mother discouraged him in no uncertain terms: "The head that contains all that law school knowledge should be put to better use than to take punches in a boxing match." Soon after, he returned to the practice of law in Washington.

In the early 1930s, Sirica helped start a boxing club and began a life-long friendship with Jack Dempsey. In fact, the former heavyweight champion was best man when

Sirica married Lucille Camalier in 1952. They had three children: John, Jr., Patricia and Eileen.

In 1944, John Sirica was employed as chief counsel for the investigation of the Federal Communications Commission. When Democratic officials tried to use pressure and dampen the investigation, he resigned with the words: "I will not be a party to a whitewash." He was sworn in as a federal district judge on April 12, 1967.

Sirica showed his stamina and character as judge. Many people left his courtroom with the impression that he was harsh in his sentencing, yet no one could say that he was not fair. But what many could not see was how he suffered in sentencing people. This was the most unpleasant part of his job. He was often unable to sleep the night before sentencing. He once said: "I hate to look at the faces of the wives or children of these defendants." He was not blind to the possibility of misjudgment. "A defendant is entitled to a fair trial, but cannot get a perfect trial. There is no such thing as a perfect trial."

For most of his career, not many people knew Judge Sirica outside Washington, but late in his life, he indisputably became a true American hero for his honesty, courage and determination. In his book, *To Get the Record Straight,* Sirica reveals how he became involved in the Watergate case.

In his five-year association with " Watergate," the quiet, self-effacing Sirica dealt with the break-in and coverup trials, the indictments, the guilty pleas and jailing of men who were among the most powerful in the nation, as well as the battle over the tapes.

At the time of the Watergate burglary on June 17, 1972, Sirica was chief of the fifteen-judge federal court of the District of Columbia, an honor that is given to the judge under age seventy who has the longest tenure. The Watergate indictments were returned to Sirica who, as chief justice, had the option of assigning the case for trial or allowing it to go into routine rotation. He assigned it to himself and handled it from the start, often becoming a quasi-prosecutor.

Sirica first tried the seven men charged with burglarizing Democratic headquarters in the Watergate. Five pleaded guilty and two were convicted. After the Senate Watergate committee learned Nixon had tape-recorded all his White House conversations, the prosecutor subpoenaed the tapes. Nixon refused to comply, and Sirica was asked to rule.

"I felt caught between two conflicting urges," Sirica said. "The first was to honor the tradition that no president had been forced to turn over documents he had decided would damage the public interest. In short, I did not want to be in the position of writing new law."

But Judge Sirica decided that examination of the tapes would be the only way to settle "the questions about Watergate that were gradually destroying the Nixon administration. I felt, to a large extent, that I was being asked to decide the fate of the Nixon presidency."

A later Sirica decision on another batch of tapes was challenged into the Supreme Court, which upheld him in the landmark "United States v. Richard Nixon" decision. Four days later, in the resulting furor, Nixon released a transcript of the tapes and resigned.

Still, Sirica felt justice was ill-served. In his memoirs, he wrote: "Nixon should have stood trial. No matter how great his personal loss, Nixon did manage to keep himself above the law. He was forced to give up his office, but he was not treated the same way as the other defendants."

Jeb Magruder, who broke Watergate and was sentenced to four years in prison, became a Presbyterian minister after his release. "I felt he treated me fairly," he said of Sirica. "You cannot ask anything else of a judge but fairness."

History records for posterity that a son of Italian immigrants held in his hands the fate of the president of the United States of America, the attorney general, and the most important members of the Nixon administration.

Colleges and universities have given Judge Sirica honorary degrees: College of New Rochelle, Brown University, New England School of Law, Fairfield University, City University of New York, Duke University, Georgetown University, Mount St. Mary's College in Maryland and Gettysburg College in Pennsylvania.

Judge Sirica was the recipient of numerous awards and honors. In 1973: Award of Merit, American Judges Association; Time Magazine "Man of the Year." In 1974:

Touchdown Club of Washington Tommie Award; The John Carroll Award, Georgetown University Alumni Association; Key West Florida, Jaycee Good Government Award; Certificate of Achievement, Italian Historical Society of America; Certificate of Outstanding Contribution to the Judiciary, Phi Alpha Delta International Law Fraternity.

In 1975: Brian McMahon Memorial Award, Fordham University Club of Washington; Outstanding Trial Judge, Association of Trial Lawyers of America; Award of Merit, Federal Administrative Law Judges' Conference; James Cardinal Gibbons Medalist, Catholic University of America Alumni Association; Award of Merit, United States Department of Justice, Drug Enforcement Administration; Award of Merit, American Justinian Society of Jurists.

Judge Sirica continued to be recognized as a distinguished member of the Judiciary. In 1976: Outstanding Achievement Award, National Association of Secondary School Principals; Italian-American Bicentennial Tribute; Award of Merit, Association of Federal Investigators Judiciary Award. In 1977: Award of Merit, American Academy of Achievement, Kappa Alpha Psi Humanitarian Award. In 1978: Award of Merit, Jewish National Fund; Award in Recognition of Outstanding and Distinguished Service by District of Columbia Bar; and the Centennial Medal, Vanderbilt University.

John J. Sirica, the federal judge whose relentless pursuit of the truth in the Watergate scandal unraveled Richard Nixon's presidency, died on August 14, 1992. He was eighty-eight years old.

References: *Current Biography,* H.W. Wilson, 1974.
            L'Italo-Americano, August 20, 1992.
            John Sirica, *To Get the Record Straight,* Norton, 1979.
            The Italian Tribune, August 20, 1992.
            Who's Who in Government, 1992-1993.

Sylvester Stallone

Sylvester Stallone's humble beginnings belie his present status of superstar, popular writer and producer of world-wide affluence. For, in fact, he was born in 1946, in the charity ward of a New York City hospital. The attendant doctor's misused forceps inflicted permanent damage to the left side of the infant's face and left him with a drooping eye and what would later turn out to be a speech impediment. (Parenthetically it must be noted that many years later, Stallone turned both defects to his advantage in portraying Rambo and other similar characters on the screen.)

His father, Francesco Stallone, was an Italian immigrant. As a shoemaker in New York City, he was hard put to provide for his family, when they lived in Hell's Kitchen. The family moved to Silver Spring, Maryland, a suburb of Washington, D.C., when Sylvester was five. There, his mother, Jacqueline, who before marriage had been a circus worker and then one of Billy Rose's long-stemmed show girls at the Diamond Horseshoe, had to settle for opening and running a beauty parlor instead. His father raised polo ponies and played a sandlot version of polo. Young Sylvester developed a kinship with horses which he indulges today with his stable of twenty and his play at the Santa Barbara Polo Club.

But the family soon disintegrated, and Sylvester spent several years in foster homes until at fifteen he went to live with his mother in a slum section of Philadelphia. Although he was expelled frequently for his delinquent behavior, his muscular physique and prowess miraculously won him an athletic scholarship to the American College in Switzerland. Subsequently, he barely made it into the University of Miami where he briefly studied drama. While there, he wrote and assiduously applied himself to curing his speech defect by reading aloud from Shakespeare into a tape recorder. He also tried his hand at a variety of jobs.

Stallone was twenty-two, when he went to New York City determined to become an actor. He initially worked as an usher, at the Baronet movie theater. Gradually he worked his way into Off-Broadway and managed to land small parts in occasional films. Finally, in 1974, he played one of the leads in the low-budget New York-made film *The Lords of Flatbush.*

After a succession of supporting roles in such Hollywood films as *Farewell My Lovely, Capone,* and *Death Race 2000,* Stallone determined to create the opportunity to become a star by writing his own screen play. He studied the necessary techniques and applied them to his own theme: a down-and-out boxer whose grit and determination make him a champion. In three days he had handwritten the script and his pregnant wife, Sasha, had typed it. Although he had less than one hundred dollars in the bank, Stallone stubbornly refused a producer's offer to buy the story outright for $150,000. He held out until his terms were accepted: he would star in his own creation.

In an article in *Cosmopolitan* (January 1990), Leo Janos called *Rocky,* "the greatest personal triumph the movie business has ever known." It won the Oscar for best picture, making Stallone an instant star and millionaire. Since then, the resourceful and irrepressible Stallone has continued to write and star in all the sequels about the small-time "Italian Stallion," a tough, honest, decent man, who gets the chance to fight the champ and triumphs against heavy odds in the killing sport of boxing. Over the years the *Rocky* sequels have grossed over 250-billion dollars, making Stallone the highest paid actor in the business and the biggest box-office draw in the world.

Stallone, as writer and actor, has created still another universally known character—Rambo—the savage, vengeance-seeking former Green Beret, who singlehandedly fought most of the North Vietnamese and Soviet armies and emerged the clear winner.

Although most of his other movies, including the recent comedy *Oscar,* have not done too well at the box office, even his severest critics must admit that with *Rocky* and *Rambo,* Stallone has created two of the most popular and controversial screen characters of this generation, embodying the ability of the average man to reach for the stars. Indeed, even the *New York Times* took a serious look at what it called "The Stallone Era" a couple of years ago, when Stallone's career hit the ten-year mark.

His phenomenal success has enabled Stallone to participate in peripheral business ventures such as the New York City restaurant "Planet Hollywood" which he and his partners, Arnold Schwarzenegger and Bruce Willis opened in 1991. A more creative outlet—painting—not only affords him other means of expression, but also a source of satisfaction. In September of 1990, the Hanson Art Galleries held an exhibit of his work. All his paintings, expressionistic in style, sold at prices ranging from $4000 to

$40,000. His artistic and his commercial successes have enabled him to dedicate time and considerable effort in support of charitable causes.

Stallone's son, Sage, seems to be following in his father's footsteps, co-starring with him in *Rocky V.* His younger son, Seargeoh, bright and active in his early years, was diagnosed as autistic when he was three. Devastated, Stallone and his wife, Sasha, traveled world-wide seeking help for their child, but to no avail. Stallone is assiduously supporting efforts to define the causes of autism and, hopefully, to discover the ultimate cure, not only for Seargeoh, but for all the other young victims to whom he is passionately committed.

References: Nancy Collins, *Cosmopolitan,* "Hard to Get, But She Got 'Em, October 1991.

John Culhane, *Reader's Digest,* "Where Great Movies Come From," February 1990.

Harper's Magazine, January 1991.

Leo Janos, *Cosmopolitan,* "Sly Stallone's Rocky Road to Happiness," January 1990.

Carol Lynn Muthers, *Redbook,* "My Sons Are My Life," December 1990.

Stephen Rebello, *Interview,* "Sly's Significant Mother," October 1990.

Paul Tagliabue

Paul Tagliabue, a senior partner at a powerful and prestigious Washington, D.C., law firm, was well aware of the problems and challenges he would face as Commissioner of the National Football League, when chosen to succeed Pete Rozelle in that capacity in November, 1989. Tagliabue's firm, Covington and Burling, had assigned him to the NFL account shortly after he became associated with them and he became Pete Rozelle's most valued outside legal counselor.

Tagliabue has accepted that challenge as he has always done in the past, with the unswerving determination to work his hardest and do his utmost to merit the responsibilities placed on him. His parents, Charles and Mary Tagliabue, had emphatically fostered the Italian work ethic in their close-knit family. When Paul John Tagliabue, the third of four sons, was born on November 24, 1940, in Jersey City, his father owned a small business doing repair work at factories and loading docks on the New Jersey waterfront. An especially hard worker himself, he set very high standards for his sons as well, emphasizing the necessity of hard work and the importance of education.

As a youngster, Paul would practice basketball for hours on an outdoor court, even when the temperature dropped below freezing. His father, a basketball player in the '20s, encouraged and helped him, but saw to it that Paul's school work did not suffer as a result.

By the time he was a sophomore at St. Michael's High School in Union City, Paul was within an inch of his adult height of six feet, five inches. He became the second-best basketball player in the school's history, and he also won the state high-jump championship in track. Because of his athletic achievements and his excellent academic record, more than two dozen colleges tried to recruit him. He chose to accept an athletic scholarship from Georgetown

University in Washington, D.C., a superior college academically, but not yet prominent in the college basketball
domain. Tagliabue played well enough on the Georgetown
team, but tore some ligaments in his knee while playing in
a summer league. With typical grit and determination, he
continued to play for Georgetown, leading the team in
rebounds for four years and becoming its captain during
his senior year.

Tagliabue did not permit his basketball activities to
impinge upon his academic standing. As a government
major, he not only made the Dean's List regularly, but was
also elected president of his senior class and was a finalist
for a Rhodes scholarship.

After graduating from Georgetown with honors in 1962,
Tagliabue won the prestigious Root-Tilden scholarship to
the New York University School of Law. While studying
there, he served as editor of the *Law Review.* He received
his law degree in 1965, and clerked for a year for Judge
Oscar Davis in the old Court of Claims in Washington,
D.C., before signing on with the State Department of Defense in September 1966, as a policy analyst on European
and North Atlantic affairs. When he resigned in 1969 to
go into private practice, he was awarded the Department's
highest civilian honor, the Meritorius Civilian Service
Medal for his studies "on the demonstrative use of nuclear
weapons and on nuclear consultation with [the United
States] allies."

Covington and Burling—the law firm Paul Tagliabue joined—is one of the most respected in Washington. He eventually became an antitrust specialist and also served on the committee which oversees the operations of the company's 275 attorneys.

Tagliabue's particular responsibility was to advise Pete Rozelle, then Commissioner of NFL, regarding the widely publicized and highly sensitive Namath-Bachelors III affair. In the course of the subsequent decade, Rozelle became the most respected commissioner in professional sports. His most valued legal counselor for twenty years, Tagliabue was hardly a household name to the average football fan; all his close work with Pete Rozelle was done behind the scenes.

Nevertheless, he was indeed privy to every major decision affecting the league from 1969 to 1989. He had dealt with its traumatic issues from the Joe Namath-Oakland Raider antitrust lawsuit to the United States Football League's antitrust lawsuit. In the latter case, particularly, Tagliabue scored a major victory when the litigants had to accept a settlement fee of one dollar.

After Pete Rozelle stepped down as commissioner of the NFL in 1989, Tagliabue was elected to that office. He resigned from his law firm, and finally emerged from behind the scenes in the football arena to demonstrate that he was resourceful, knowledgeable, and more than capable of overseeing the league's expansion into international markets. In a short time he put his stamp on the league—from T-shirts to TV contracts—and has involved himself at every level, from finance, to broadcast, to labor. This involvement was sure to grow and, only a year after his election, the league approved a sweeping reorganization that invested him with more direct authority than Rozelle ever visualized. At present, all the league's committees report to Tagliabue directly, rather than through the various owners. The latter do not object, impressed as they are with the commissioner's greatest accomplishment so far—a record TV package worth $3.6 billion over four years.

Another high priority on the agenda is to cultivate the growing international interest in American football; he has added an annual pre-season game in Berlin to complement the games played every August in Tokyo and in London. Responding to growing public concern, Paul Tagliabue has also reformed and enforced the league's drug-testing policies, increased the emphasis on drug-rehabilitation programs, and instituted tough new guidelines for steroid testing. He is also an outspoken supporter of hiring policies that would open up more NFL coaching opportunities to blacks.

Clearly, Tagliabue's responsibilities are herculean, his aspirations for the league are boundless, and there are never enough hours in the day. Although he maintains that a person should be "consumed" by his job, his colleagues and friends insist that his foremost priority is his family. He and his wife, the former Chandler Minter of

Georgia, who had come to New York as a graduate student in English, and whom he married on August 28, 1965, now live in New York City, just two blocks from NFL headquarters. Their children—Emily, a student at Yale University; and Drew, an Amherst student who spent his junior year in Japan—are very close to their parents and relatives, and equally committed to the importance and necessity of family, education, and work.

References: Dave Anderson, *The New York Times*, "Tagliabue Has Only Begun to Rebound," October 29, 1989.
Current Biography, H.W. Wilson, 1992.
Gerald Eskenazi, *The New York Times,* "Tagliabue Sweeps into Action," October 28, 1990.
Peter Finch, *Business Week*, "Tagliabue Is Everywhere But in the Huddle," January 28, 1991.
Thomas George, *The New York Times*, "Tagliabue Is Elected NFL Commissioner," October 27, 1989.
Robert Thomas, Jr., *The New York Times*, "Family Man, Sports Fan, NFL Chief," October 27, 1989.
Telander, Rick, *Sports Illustrated*, "The Face of the Sweeping Change," September 10, 1990.

Daniel J. Travanti, Jr.

Television and motion-picture actor Daniel John Travanti was born in Kenosha, Wisconsin, March 7, 1941, to immigrant Italian parents. Both Elvira DeAngelis and Giovanni Travanti were from Ascoli Piceno, in the Marche region.

Dan Travanti always knew he would be an actor, even though no one in his family had any connection with the profession. In high-school he was an all-American football star, but turned down athletic scholarships from the University of Notre Dame, and from Marquette, Wisconsin, and Boston College. After winning four high-school speech contests and being a finalist twice in national high-school competition, he was offered the top academic scholarships of Princeton, Dartmouth and Harvard Universities.

Travanti chose to attend the University of Wisconsin as a Woodrow Wilson Fellow, graduating in three years while earning every academic honor including Phi Beta Kappa; he acted there in five major productions and in numerous other offerings. He also worked in summer stock in Beloit, Wisconsin, in 1961 and 1962, appearing in sixteen plays. After graduating, he attended the Yale School of Drama for one year, acting in all four major productions and in over fifty classroom "scenes." In addition, he worked at the Montowese Summer Theater, appearing in seven plays. That winter, Travanti acted at the Cleveland Playhouse. He then served six months in the U.S. Army and five more years in the Army Reserves.

He went to New York in 1963, and has earned his living as an actor ever since. He appeared in sixty television series, two daytime soap operas, three films and in one television series as a regular.

Dan Travanti played Octavius Caesar in *Antony and Cleopatra* in Los Angeles (1965). In 1972 and 1973, he toured with Sada Thompson in *Twigs,* a Broadway play. In 1977, he played Petruchio in *The Taming of the Shrew* at the Old Globe Theater in San Diego.

For his work in "Hill Street Blues," Travanti received two Emmys as Outstanding Lead Actor in a Drama Series. In 1982, he received the Golden Globe Award from the Hollywood Foreign Press Association. As Captain Frank Furillo, Travanti, according to fans and critics, has created one of the most positive portrayals of an Italian-American in television history.

Dan starred with Edward Asner in *A Case of Libel,* a made for cable movie, for which he was nominated for Ace Award's Outstanding Actor in a Lead Film Role. That same year, 1983, he appeared in an NBC film, *Adam,* and received another Emmy nomination and the Isaac Hecker Award, presented for this performance and his work as Captain Furillo, for "performances that enrich and humanize audiences." The Isaac Hecker Award is a presentation of the Paulists who also bestow the Humanitas Awards each year for outstanding writing for television.

In 1985 Dan played Edward R. Murrow in the HBO film, *Murrow,* and was nominated a second time for the Ace Award as Outstanding Actor. In 1986 Dan appeared again as John Walsh in a film made for NBC, *Adam: His Song Continues.*

After the release of *Aurora*, a movie set in Italy and co-starring Sophia Loren, Travanti was chosen "Man of the Year" by the Italian T.V. magazine *Sorrisi e Canzoni*, one of Italy's largest publications.

Travanti lives in Pacific Palisades, California, with two dogs and three cats. Active as he is in his acting career and attendant professional commitments, Travanti makes time to work for the cause of abused children. This was acknowledged by the NIAF when he received his Artistic Achievement Award. He is equally bound to the problem of missing children. Indeed, his television movie, *Adam*, explored the plight not only of kidnapped children, but of their bereaved parents as well.

Dan Travanti filmed *Midnight Crossing*, with Faye Dunaway and Kim Cattrall, in 1987. From September 1987, through January 1988, he toured in *I Never Sang for My Father.* The play now appears on the PBS series, *American Playhouse.*

Travanti co-starred with Kris Kristofferson and Cheryl Ladd in *Millennium,* for Twentieth Century-Fox, which was released at Christmas, 1987. In July he was a judge at an international film festival in Gijon, Spain.

In the spring of 1989, he was a guest performer at "The Prince's Trust," the favorite charity of Prince Charles, at London's Palladium Theater. He filmed *Fellow Traveller*, BBC-HBO movie, which aired in March 1990. He also played Joe Hynes in an NBC film, *Howard Beach: Making the Case for Murder.*

In December and January (1989-1990), Dan Travanti was a Catskill comic in *Only Kidding,* at the Cleveland Playhouse. Later, he went to London, to play Valmont in the Royal Shakespeare Company production of *Les Liaisons Dangereuses.*

After fifteen weeks with this RSC production, he played the title role in a movie for U.S.A. Cable, *Tagget.* Toward the end of 1990, Travanti played Roy Boxter in *Eyes of the Witness,* for CBS. His most recent portrayals are: *Weep No More, My Lady,* Canal Plus, France; *The Christmas Stallion,* Wales Television; *Hello, Stranger,* Irish Television, and *No Room For Opal,* Boston Television, Channel 5. Considering his sustained excellence of performance in each of these, Travanti can be expected to continue entertaining audiences for many years to come.

References: Christopher P. Andersen, *The New Book of People,* 1986.
Who's Who in Entertainment, 1989-1990.

John A. Volpe

Initially schooled as an architectural engineer, this multi-faceted Italian-American, with incredibly hard work and highly principled efforts, founded The Volpe Company, a successful multinational corporation, and subsequently found fulfillment and honor in an active and diversified political career.

In fact, John Volpe was elected to serve three terms as Governor of Massachusetts. His achievements are all the more remarkable in view of his modest background.

Born in Wakefield, Massachusetts, December 8, 1908, John was the second of five children of Vito and Filomena Benedetto, who had emigrated from the Abruzzi region in Italy. His father, a laborer in the building trade, eventually became a master craftsman and the community leader in Malden.

Because of economic pressures, from age eleven John worked after school, averaging about four dollars a week. When a financial family crisis occurred, he had to change his plans to attend a prestigious college. As a senior in Malden High School, he switched from the college preparatory course to the technical, and registered at Wentworth Institute for the fall-session evening courses.

He worked for his fathers' newly organized Volpe & Son Company and, in 1933, became head of his own business. He married Jennie Benedetto in 1934. Six years later, he won the bid for a million-dollar job—a post-office garage in South Boston.

In 1943, John Volpe volunteered for the Seabees. He received a commission as Lieutenant Junior Grade. Two brothers followed him into the Seabees, another joined the regular Navy, and even his father volunteered for civilian duty with the Coast Guard.

In Camp Peary, Virginia, he trained sailors for work in construction battalions. Forty-eight of his class of 60 graduated and became Drill Instructors. He organized a brass marching band, much as his father had done with Italian immigrants in Boston.

Lieutenant Volpe never did get to the Pacific; he was sent instead to Washington, D.C., to interview officer candidates for the Civil Engineer Corps. When the War ended, he was still with the Bureau of Naval Personnel. Upon his release to inactive duty, he returned to Malden where a building boom was in progress. The Volpe Company was reopened. By virtue of its technical excellence and its high standards for safety, in school and hospital buildings particularly, it flourished. In country-wide speeches, Volpe emphasized the humanitarian aspects of accident prevention that would lower insurance costs and affect the winning or the losing of a bid.

Volpe's real break came in 1951 when Sinclair Weeks, the Massachusetts committeeman in control of the Republican Party, chose him as one of his deputy chairmen. Volpe rose in the Republican ranks.

Soon John Volpe was appointed Commissioner of the Department of Public Works in Massachusetts and, with characteristic energy and dedication, he reorganized the department and reformed its practices. In 1956, during Eisenhower's administration, he served as the first federal highway administrator.

Back again in private life, he opened two branches of his company: in Miami and Washington, D.C. Politically active in a run for the governorship of Massachusetts, he was staunch against the inevitable machinations of political campaigning. He persisted in his idealistic conviction that "if honest men did nothing, government would be left to the dishonest." He won his first gubernatorial election in 1960; again in 1964, and also 1966. He restructured the Department of Public Works, improved programs for mental health and higher education and tackled the monumental problems of auto insurance and the question of the death penalty. His energy, dedication and resourcefulness won the attention of several political leaders in Washington.

With his appointment by President Richard Nixon to the Cabinet position of Secretary of the newly formed Department of Transportation, John Volpe, a Republican who had served three terms in traditionally Democratic Massachusetts, became the second Italian-American to hold a Cabinet position. To preclude the possibility of conflict of interest, he sold all his shares in the Volpe Co., and his name was taken off the company's designation.

Volpe's practice of reading everything he signed made him aware of several serious political problems, such as, in the civil-rights and the inner-city highway crisis areas. These were his top priorities. Another focus was on redressing the imbalance between the automobile and public transportation.

His projects ended in 1972 when President Nixon, after his overwhelming victory, reorganized his Cabinet. Volpe was offered the Ambassadorship to Italy. He settled in Rome, with his wife and son Jack, to a very different assignment and environment.

Though living in baronial surroundings at the Embassy Residence in Rome, Volpe traveled to factory towns, southern villages and large industrial centers for more meaningful communication with the natives. Italy was plagued with the threat of terrorism and natural disasters, such as, earthquakes and floods. During his four-year service at the Embassy, he coped with all these emergencies so well that he became known as the "activist ambassador."

After his return to Boston, Ambassador Volpe took a brief whirl at the lecture circuit. He became an active member of the National Italian American Foundation, serving for three years as its President. Besides being honored by this organization, Volpe received thirty-four honorary degrees from American colleges and universities. He served in the capacity of Chairman of the National Governors' Conference, and also President of the Council of State Governments.

Ambassador Volpe holds the Italian Order of Merit and two Orders from the Vatican as a Knight of Malta and Knight Commander of the Holy Sepulcher. His incredible zeal, energy, and versatility have marked his every endeavor.

References: Kathleen Kilgore, *John Volpe: The Life of an Immigrant's Son,* Yankee Books, 1987.
Who's Who in Government, 1973.

Index

Fashion, 14, 16; Fishing, 49; Food and Nutrition, 160, 177, 193; Metallurgy, 62
Israel, 192
Italy, 2, 24, 27, 31, 36, 62, 73, 82, 92, 95, 99, 110, 116, 123-25, 128, 146, 156-57, 160, 163, 169, 175, 177, 192, 219, 222; Sicily, 48, 182

Kennedy, John F. (President), 26, 156
Kent State Univ., 138
Kmart (S.S. Kresge), 12-16
Knights of Columbus, 196
Kouver, Elliot, 4
Kristofferson, Kris, 216

L

J

Jackson, Reggie, 52
James, Harry, 188, 190
Jamestown (VA), viii
Janos, Leo, 204
Japan, 188, 191, 212
Jefferson, Thomas, 125, 127
Jenkins, Gordon, 191
Jeno F. Paulucci & Assoc. of Florida, Inc., 161
Jersey City (NJ), 44, 208
John Carroll Univ., 24
Johnson, Lyndon (President), 26, 156, 163, 176
Jordan, Michael, 21
Judiciary and Judgeship, 23, 25-26, 168, 185, 187, 197, 200

K

Kazan, Elia, 192
Kennedy Center for the Performing Arts, 98, 146, 192

Labor and Labor Unions, 43, 67-72, 177, 210
Ladd, Cheryl, 216
Ladd, Diane, 3
Law, 24, 29, 43, 154, 183-85, 196, 200, 207, 209; Constitutional, 185
Leaver, Linda, 19
Lee, Spike, 3
Legislation: Civil Rights Act of 1966, 170; Columbus Day, 170; Equal Rights Amendment, 10; Immigration Reform and Control Act (1966), 170; Philadelphia Plan (1969), 170; Racial Segregation (1954), 43
Lehigh Univ., 102
Lincoln, Abraham, 57
Literacy, 135
Literature, viii, 91, 93-94; Playwright, 141
Logan, Greg, 134
Logan, Joshua, 54
Lollobrigida, Gina, 110
London (England), 148, 150, 211, 216
Loren, Sophia, x, 108-14, 216
Luigino's, Inc., 160